100 Ideas for Secondary Teachers

Revision

John Mitchell

Other titles in the 100 Ideas for Secondary Teachers series:

100 Ideas for Secondary Teachers

Revision

John Mitchell

BLOOMSBURY

LONDON • OXFORD • NEW YORK • NEW DELHI • SYDNEY

Bloomsbury Education
An imprint of Bloomsbury Publishing Plc

50 Bedford Square   1385 Broadway
London   New York
WC1B 3DP   NY 10018
UK   USA

www.bloomsbury.com

Bloomsbury is a registered trade mark of Bloomsbury Publishing Plc

First published 2016

British Library Cataloguing-in-Publication Data
A catalogue record for this book is available from the British Library.

ISBN: PB: 9781472913753
      ePub: 9781472913777
      ePDF: 9781472913760

Library of Congress Cataloging-in-Publication Data
A catalog record for this book is available from the Library of Congress.

10 9 8 7 6 5 4 3 2 1

Typeset by Newgen Knowledge Works (P) Ltd, Chennai, India
Printed and bound in CPI Group (UK) Ltd, Croydon, CR0 4YY

This book is produced using paper that is made from wood grown
in managed, sustainable forests. It is natural, renewable and
recyclable. The logging and manufacturing processes conform
to the environmental regulations of the country of origin.

To view more of our titles please visit www.bloomsbury.com

This book is dedicated to the people who started it all and supported me every step of the way, my parents – Dennis and Monica.

Also to the memory of Ronald Britten (1929–2013) – history teacher, mentor, guide and, most importantly of all, friend.

Contents

Acknowledgements

Although it is my name on the front of this book, this is the work of a huge cast of people who have influenced, contributed and supported me over the past two decades.

Professionally, thank you to all the people who have had a positive influence on my career, so far spanning over 15 years in Hertfordshire and Merseyside. I have had the pleasure of working with many inspirational educators who have given me great advice and support, and their influence runs throughout this book. Although I cannot name you all it would be wrong for me not to mention 'The Riser Crew', particularly James, Lauren, Luke, Liz and Stanbo, who regularly accompany me for a real ale or a cider, and put up with my flights of fancy after a busy working day in the classroom.

Outside of this sphere, I would like to pay full recognition to my virtual PLN (Professional Learning Network). My contributions via Twitter and my blog – www.jivespin.wordpress.com – have led directly to the writing of this book, something I would not imagined doing a few years ago. Without your dialogue, feedback and banter, I would be a less effective teacher and so I thank you for that.

Members of this PLN have contributed directly and indirectly to this book by freely giving advice as well as being guest authors and writing an idea or two, and they deserve huge thanks for their generosity amidst their very busy workloads that my request added to. Sophie Scott – @binarygenius – wrote Ideas 99 and 100 drawing upon her extensive knowledge of using technology in teaching.

A massive bunch of flowers must go to Holly Gardner at Bloomsbury Publishing, who first asked me to write this book and whose wise guidance and faith were vital in this process. Without you, this book would never have reached the proposal stage let alone being published. Also, Sam Hartburn, who edited this book and made me look much better than I really am.

However, the most profound thanks must go to my family – my parents, Dennis and Monica, and my brothers, Dave and Paul. Who would have thought a working class boy who went to a condemned school from Hemel Hempstead (pronounced 'emel 'empstead) would have a book to their name? It is with your support that I do.

Introduction

The very word revision can strike fear into the heart of every classroom. Revision is associated with stressful periods of preparation for examinations of any shape and size, the cramming of knowledge, (which may lead to young brains exploding at any moment), and teachers collapsing due to the increasing demand for them to prepare young people for the constant cycle of examinations provided by the modern education system.

It does not have to be like this. With careful planning and by using exciting and engaging activities, revision can be an enjoyable and engrossing process where you can see students' progress at the end of every lesson. I hope this book will help you to plan an engaging and effective revision programme with a series of lessons that will help your students prepare for any examinations or assessments that they might face. This book is also mindful of the fact that revision should not be restricted to public exam preparation (although this is an important part of the book), and thus many of these activities and ideas are also suitable for reviewing work and preparing students for internal assessments. Therefore, I hope there is something for every teacher in this toolkit of ideas.

The ideas in this book are organised around common themes, which will help you to locate ideas that are relevant or applicable to the content you wish to cover in your session. Many of the activities and ideas require limited (if any!) preparation, which is a godsend for the typical teacher, who has an ever-increasing workload and other pressures, such as constantly changing exam specifications, to cope with.

There is a hashtag linked to each idea in the book. I would be very interested to hear how you take these ideas forward, in addition to the impact they have in your classroom and, more importantly, on your students. Therefore, I strongly encourage you to share how you use these ideas by using both the book's main hashtag, #100ideas and the hashtag linked with a specific idea. Of course, feel free to tweet me directly at @Jivespin.

I look forward to hearing from you.

John

How to use this book

This book includes quick, easy, practical ideas for you to dip in and out of, that will support you in planning and carrying out an effective revision programme.

Each idea includes:

- A catchy title, that is easy to refer to and share with your colleagues.
- A quote from a teacher or student describing their experiences of the idea or a problem they may have had that using the idea solved.
- A summary of the idea in bold, making it easy to flick through the book and identify an idea you want to use at a glance.
- A step-by-step guide to implementing the idea.

Each idea also includes one or more of the following:

Teaching tip

Some extra advice on how or how not to run the activity or put the strategy into practice.

Taking it further

Ideas and advice for how to extend the idea or develop it further.

Bonus idea ★

There are 29 bonus ideas in this book that are extra exciting and extra original.

Online resources also accompany this book. When the link to the resource is referenced in the book, follow the link, http://goo.gl/iQMcpE, to find extra resources, catalogued under the relevant idea number.

Share how you use these ideas in the classroom and find out what other teachers have done by using **#100ideas** and the other hashtags given in the book.

The big picture – whole-school issues

Part 1

Revision charter

We work as a team. That means doing everything I say!

Highlighting and re-emphasising your expectations for students in context at the beginning of a revision programme reminds them what they are required to do to prepare for their exams and how we will support them during this stressful period.

#RevisionCharter

A revision charter lists the actions and responsibilities of students and staff, provides a plan of action to support your students, and also restates your expectations. Here is an example:

Revision charter

You should prepare for revision sessions by:

- reading around revision topics in advance;
- noting down new terms, names and dates;
- noting down anything you do not understand;
- keeping notes up to date.

During the revision sessions, you should:

- pay attention and listen;
- ask questions when you don't understand;
- take part in revision activities as best you can;
- help others where appropriate.

After the revision sessions, you should:

- revise notes and ensure there are no gaps;
- re-read your notes after a few weeks;
- add relevant handouts to notes and ensure that they are organised logically;
- highlight or underline key points.

Your teacher will:

- cover relevant topics and provide materials;
- teach using mark schemes and past papers;
- provide examination details;
- recommend extra reading;
- be on hand for advice.

What's in your revision toolkit?

Be prepared!

Preparing an effective revision mindset and programme is crucial for exam success. This introductory exercise shows students what they need to consider when undertaking a rigorous, yet realistic, revision programme.

This flexible activity helps students to develop their own revision toolkit for learning and reviewing work, and can be applied in a number of ways.

One way is to create a bag of items that each represent a feature of effective revision. Ask a volunteer to choose an item and explain what they think it represents. For example:

- Bottle of water – hydrating the brain is crucial when revising.
- Map – effective revision must follow a plan; you must know where you are going, how you are going to get there, and what you need to achieve.
- Sweatband – exercise and physical activity helps keep you fit and energised for learning.
- Fruit – keeps you healthy and is good for the brain.
- A clock – time management is crucial for effective revision.
- Picture of a handshake – revision can be a collaborative activity.

Another way to use this idea is to give your students an outline of an empty bag on a sheet of A3 paper. Ask students to draw items in their bag with that they think represent great revision. They must explain their choices. This can then be presented to the rest of the class in a plenary activity. This activity is particularly effective in tutor periods or PSHE (Personal, Social and Health Education) lessons.

Teaching tip

The revision toolkit principle makes for a very effective assembly for students who are preparing for examinations at any level. This idea is one for heads of year to consider in their year assembly timetable.

Taking it further

Extend the activity by explaining to students that there is a hole in their revision toolkit and they can only save three items. Which items would they want to save and why? This question gets students to think about prioritising the most important elements of exam preparation.

#RevisionToolkit

3

Feedback or feedforward?

Consistently high-quality marking and constructive feedback from teachers ensures that pupils make rapid gains.

The influential works of Wiliam, Black and Hattie have all emphasised that quality feedback is central to student progress and raising standards. With OFSTED's increasing focus on feedback and creating a learning dialogue, never before has teacher feedback been under such scrutiny.

The broad model of feedback which many schools follow is based upon Black and Wiliam's 'medal and mission' approach. The 'medal' relates to any positive attention, while the 'mission' refers feedback that targets further development and progress. The assessment strategies that follow this broad model emphasise 'feedforward' rather than 'feedback' – the teacher focuses on how the student should progress forward rather than looking back on what they have done wrong.

Hattie's research shows that comment-only marking is the most effective form of feedback. Grades and marks encourage students to compare with each other and consequently focus less on what they need to do next to make progress, while comment-only feedback encourages them to focus on improvement. Here are a few 'medal and mission' ideas, with a focus upon comment-only feedback, to enhance your revision programme.

Mock exam feedback form Rather than just handing students back their scripts, give them a mock exam feedback form. Include a breakdown of their results by paper, an overall grade, two points that they did well and two targets for each paper, and a space for their feedback and feedforward – what they are going to do to help meet these targets. Ask students to stick the sheets into their exercise books.

Verbal feedback stamp When you give verbal feedback, stamp the work and ask the student to write down your comments. This strategy allows for one-to-one guidance and gives personalised feedback, which Hattie argues is the most effective form of feedback. This is also an easy and time-effective way of logging a learning dialogue.

'Two stars and a wish' and 'Even better if . . .' These make very effective feedback frames, either verbal or written. The 'two stars and a wish frame' is one where you highlight two areas where the work was good (the two stars) and give one piece of advice of how it can be improved (a wish). You can buy stamps bearing the slogans to speed up the marking process.

One-word targets To save time without compromising on standards, introduce a one-word-target marking list for each revision assessment, tailored to students' performance. This strategy gives evidence of learning feedback, student progress and effective use of DIRT (Directed Improvement and Reflection Time). Give students a list of words with their target definitions; the words can be taken from the exam mark scheme. Link each target to a task, to be completed in lessons. For example: *Explanation* – although your work showed good knowledge, it was too descriptive to reach the higher grades. To improve further, you need to consider applying your knowledge to help explain your points. Use the 'explanation sentence starters' sheet in your book to do this. Practise by writing a paragraph on mass production, which is relevant to the essay question, using at least TWO of these sentence starters.

Sticky notes While students are working, you may spot an error or a tweak needed for development. Instead of interrupting students, write formative feedback on a sticky note and give it to them. Ask students to copy their sticky note feedback into their book when they've finished the work – another way of providing a learning dialogue.

#Feedback

Revision log

Revision log. Stardate 2014. We have entered the revision zone . . .

Keeping a check on independent revision can be difficult. This handy little tool can help you do this easily and with little effort.

#Revisionlog

One way of monitoring students' independent revision and establishing good revision habits is to use a tool produced by Dale Banham for the Schools History Project. Originally intended as a monitoring form for independent learning, the questions asked are pertinent for independent revision.

The form requires students to consider five questions that relate to revision they are doing outside the classroom:

- **Research** How have you prepared for the revision topics this week? What methods have you used?
- **Read Around** What books/materials have you read as part of your revision programme this week? How have you recorded your work?
- **Review** How have you reviewed the work from your revision sessions last week? Have you converted your notes into a revision resource?
- **Respond** How have you responded to the feedback that you have received recently?
- **Reflect** How confident are you that you are effectively preparing for the exams?

For each question students should record:

- the time spent;
- evidence of what they have done;
- feedback to the teacher, considering how they have found revision of specific topics and what additional support they may need.

Find a copy of the form at jivespin.wordpress. com/2013/09/19/independent-learning-grid/.

Revision timetables

Fail to plan. Plan to fail.

Planning revision timetables is crucial when preparing for exams. However, students can easily take so much time creating revision timetables that they run out of time to revise effectively.

Here are a few pointers to remind students of what a revision timetable should include.

- **Keep a revision diary** Advise students to map out weekly goals to help build in a sense of achievement, develop a positive mindset and maintain motivation.
- **Use broad blocking** Ask students to identify the broad topics that need greater attention over a longer period rather than planning hour-by-hour coverage of significant topics.
- **Alternate** Suggest that students balance revision of topics that they enjoy alongside topics they dislike. This makes the less popular topics more manageable and avoids underpreparation and last minute cramming.
- **Use variety** Students revising on a long term basis will easily get bored and switch off. Training students in a variety of revision activities will enable them to become effective independent learners.
- **Include others** Encourage students to share their learning experiences with their friends or parents (see Idea 78).
- **Be creative** Encourage students to make time in their revision timetable to create revision aids, such as flashcards, mind maps and flow charts, which they can revisit time and time again. The very act of creating such revision aids is brilliant revision in itself.

Teaching tip

It often falls to the pastoral team, such as heads of year and form tutors, to help students create revision timetables, usually as part of the PSHE provision. Rather than tackle this at Key Stage 4, I often prompt students to think about it at Key Stage 3 when they prepare for the school's internal examinations. Getting the students to think about how to create a revision timetable together early means that many of the common errors are ironed out long before they need to think about examinations.

#Revisiontimetable

Positive thinking

It is your attitude, not your aptitude, that determines your altitude.

Maintaining a positive learning atmosphere is always an important aspect of a teacher's work but never more so than during a revision programme, where the stakes are high.

As teachers, an important part of our job during the revision process is to act as a sponge, soaking up the negative energy that some students display and encouraging a 'you can do it!' attitude. This is becoming increasingly difficult as exams become more important, with schools and teachers being judged largely on exam results. Here are some ideas to promote positive triggers and rewards.

Get students to consider interim rewards when revising. When they are constructing a revision timetable, ensure that they programme regular breaks between revision sessions. In that break encourage a reward – this could range from a favourite snack to watching a favourite programme. Model this in lessons by regularly giving 'brain breaks' in revision sessions. (See Idea 55 for useful activities).

Encourage your students to exercise. Revision must not mean being cooped up in one room for long periods. The old maxim of a healthy mind, healthy body always rings true.

In lessons, promote the intrinsic rewards of studying your subject by highlighting what students get from the task itself, as well as its external rewards. Do this with enthusiastic presentation of the task, clearly outlining objectives linking to the exam but also emphasising how this can help with other exams and how the information and skills developed will be useful in the future.

Bonus idea ★

In revision sessions, try to give five positive and constructive comments for each negative comment. This can be difficult when the pressure is on in the run up to the exams. As an aid, have some reward stickers printed that focus on specific skills and effort, to reward students for particularly good revision work. Alongside this, use reward stamps, and reinforce the message with positive phone calls home to parents. You will be surprised at the impact this has on student motivation, regardless of age.

#Positiverevision

Positive revision habits

Turning a negative into a positive.

All students will have negative thoughts and fears during exam preparation. Helping them to confront this negativity is essential to helping them mature and develop. These ideas from the University of the First Age are perfect in achieving this.

This session should begin with a brainstorm of negative questions that students often ask in learning situations and, more specifically, revision. List these in a table with two columns.

The second stage is to turn negative questions into positive ones. Record these in the opposite column, such as:

Negative learning question	Positive learning question
Why is this work so boring?	How can I make this work more interesting?
Why did I get this lower grade than I was expecting?	What do I need to do to improve?
Why can't I remember this information?	What techniques do I need to try to improve my memory?

In the third stage of this activity, ask students to work in pairs and choose the three positive questions drawn from the second stage of the activity which are most relevant to them. They should then plan a way of answering those questions as part of their revision programme. This sequence of discussions and questions helps students to develop a growth mindset – essential for positivity and progress. It also helps to emphasise the importance of self-belief, confidence and how this can influence learning.

Teaching tip

Tackling negative thoughts may be best done in PSHE lessons or tutor periods, because you may not have time in subject-specific lessons.

Also, these groups tend to be with students who know each other well, because they spend more time together than those in subject lessons. This can engender more open discussions about negative feelings.

Taking it further

Take a picture of the board when you have completed the table at the end of the second stage. Type each positive question out onto a separate sheet of A4 paper and display them in your classroom. Constantly refer to these questions with your students during the revision period, reinforcing positive thinking and growth mindset.

#Revisionhabits

Boosting self-confidence

One important key to success is self-confidence. An important key to self-confidence is preparation.

One of the major causes of exam stress is students' fear of losing control and being unable to cope with exam pressures. A revision programme should be to promote self-confidence and build an 'I can do this!' attitude.

- Help students with setting realistic, but ambitious, manageable targets. This might be aiming for a specific mark in a quick knowledge test, or setting deadlines when creating revision resources.
- Encourage students to keep a revision journal or planner that records all their targets, when they need to achieve them by, and when they are achieved. Ask students to record an achievement every day, no matter how small. This will boost self-confidence, track progress, and improve students' self-management skills.
- Remove the word 'failure' from your vocabulary. Present mistakes as an opportunity to improve.
- Make time to celebrate progress and short-term achievements. Introduce specific rewards to celebrate good work and good attitudes. Introduce 'Revision answer of the day' and 'Revision Guru of the week' stickers. Explain why you have awarded the stickers, emphasising work and attitudes that all your students should emulate.
- Promote collaborative revision methods both in and out of the classroom. The image of revision as a lonely business should be dispelled with your students. There are many collaborative revision methods in this book that can be used so that students feel less isolated.

Bonus idea ★

Visually boost self-confidence in your classroom by putting up motivational posters and referring to them in lessons – be relentless in encouraging your students that they can be successful in your exam. There are many posters you can download from the Internet after a quick Google search. However, if you are a little more ambitious, you can make your own using apps such as Phoster or Comic Life.

#Revisionconf

Independent learning

Do it yourself!

Developing students' independence is an integral part of any revision programme. Indeed, Ofsted inspections look for this as an important element of the outstanding judgement, so signs of independence can be important indicators of exam success.

Caroline Bentley-Davies provides signs of successful independent learning which provide a framework to work within.

- **Engage in debate and discussion**. Encourage this by posing exam questions and discussing how to tackle them.
- **Ask questions of themselves and others**. Develop this through peer-assessment activities and using question board displays.
- **Speculate about the session's link with prior learning**. Revision lesson content can be plotted within the course through mind mapping.
- **Are able to make links with other subjects**. Explicit links can be made with both content and skills, especially with the growing emphasis of the core skills of literacy and numeracy across exam subjects.
- **Happily work independently, in pairs and in a variety of group situations.** Many of the activities in this book promote this.
- **Are resourceful and can find out things for themselves.** Stretch and challenge activities, such as 'Runaround' (Idea 28), develop this.
- **Enjoy and relish a challenge.** Emphasise that mistakes do not matter if you learn from them.
- **Review and reflect upon their learning.** Regularly allow DIRT in revision sessions, such as responding to feedback activities.
- **Can articulate what the next goal is and how to get there.** Develop this by using mark schemes and testing the knowledge of what is required to get to each level.

Teaching tip

Fostering independence ensures that exam success is more likely, and also prepares students for the next level of exams, whether that is AS, A2, higher or further education, all of which require an increased level of independent thinking and self-management.

Bonus idea ★

The 3B4ME strategy refers to the three different stages students should go through before coming to you for help. The three stages are Brain, Book and Buddy. Brain refers to thinking about what they know already. Book refers to the material they have got already. This could be textbook, exercise book or wall displays. Buddy refers to asking a friend or teaching assistant for guidance. If students have gone through all these stages and still do not understand then they can ask you for help.

#Indrev

Eat that Frog!

If the first thing that you do when you wake up in the morning is to eat a live frog you'll have the satisfaction of knowing that's probably going to be the worst thing that's going to happen to you all day long.

The Eat that Frog! principle of time management was created by Brain Tracy. The live frog represents the most boring task that will evoke the most procrastination. Tracy argues that if you get the 'live frog' task done first, it will improve effectiveness and boost self-confidence.

Teaching tip

Quite often the hardest part of completing this activity is for students to think of the non-required tasks that are relevant in a revision programme. Therefore, if you are using this time management strategy with a tutor group of students who are studying a whole host of subjects, it may be wise to ask the heads of department to suggest some non-required tasks for students in their subject. You can list these and give them to students for this activity.

When it comes to revising, you can break down tasks into two broad groups. The first is *Required Work*: tasks set by the teacher, which have a fixed deadline, such as set questions to be answered, essays, and preparation for practical tasks completed in lessons. The second is *Non-Required Work*: tasks with no set deadline and which are often not formally checked in lessons, such as note taking, extra independent reading and practice questions. Students often see the second group as the 'live frog' tasks. Both types of tasks are essential for reaching the higher grades but, more often than not, the non-required work is neglected by students. It is these tasks that make the difference between an average grade and an excellent grade.

The key here is to encourage your students to complete the non-required work and make it a priority. One way of doing this is to assist your students to identify non-required work for each subject and list them in a table. It could look something like this:

Subject	Non-required tasks	Time to be completed
English	• Write a synopsis on an exam text. • Practice writing PEEL paragraphs.	
History	• Read extra articles on the reign of Henry VIII. • Learn key dates of the reign of Elizabeth I.	
German	• Practice vocabulary relating to shopping. • Record speaking sentences about sports.	

Ensure that your students know that the non-required tasks are essential and relevant to their revision, take no longer than half an hour, and are realistic in their objectives. Then ask the students to plan these non-required tasks into their revision timetable, with the objective of completing one non-required task per subject per week, each one with a specifically planned timeframe in the revision timetable, for example, *Thursday 10th April between 4:00pm and 4:30pm.* These timings can be included on the table of non-required tasks, as well as on the student's overall revision timetable plan.

The benefits of supporting your students in planning their revision timetable and managing their time in this way are manifold, as it encourages students to become more independent, it encompasses the inclusion of a wider set of higher-order skills within a revision programme, and it ensures that the students are not entirely dependent upon their subject teachers.

Taking it further

The Eat that Frog! analogy is definitely worth sharing with your students when trying to get the message across about effective time management skills and tackling those less-than-attractive tasks which make up part of every revision programme. This could be a focus for an assembly ensuring that all students get that message, and it could be built upon in subsequent PSHE lessons and tutor periods.

#Eatthatfrog

Student leadership

I don't need you anymore, Miss, I can do it myself!

To successfully sit an exam, students must have a degree of independence and rely on their own resources.

#Revleadership

Let's face it, once students are in that exam hall, they are on their own. We have done all that we can for them – and probably more. We cannot sit the exam for them or tell them the answers.

The work of Graham Tyrer and Jackie Beere, promotes specifically defined roles for students in the classroom, to foster leadership skills and improve the quality of independent learning. Some of these roles include:

- **Learning reporters** These students compile a report about the key learning and revision points of the lesson. This might focus on content, exam technique or mark schemes.
- **Revision celebrators** These students highlight three things others have done well such as given a good answer or made a fantastic revision resource.
- **Revision literacy checker** These students highlight key words, as well as any mistakes in the lesson. You can deliberately make a couple of literacy errors to see if the checkers spot them.
- **Revision target planners** These students choose an aspect or several aspects of learning to revise during the lesson – this may relate to content or how to answer a type of question. At set points, ask them how well the class is working towards the chosen target. The target planner should only name students who are working well; no negative points should be directed at any individual. Also, target planners must suggest ways to improve in order to reach the target.

Supporting parents and carers

Revision begins at home.

Parents and carers are a critical ally in preparing students for a revision programme. Although our students must be the central focus, it is important not to neglect preparing parents for what can be a stressful time at home.

It is easy to overlook the fact that many parents haven't experienced preparing students for exams before. We need to assist them in supporting their childrens' revision at home so that they can reach their maximum potential. Here are a few strategies.

- At the beginning of the year, hold a Focus Evening where you share the plan for the year, with key dates relating to exams and 'revision events', such as after school revision classes.
- Use the school's VLE (Virtual Learning Environment) to communicate key exam information to parents, such as the exam boards for each subject, the names of the courses and the key topics to be revised.
- Use parents' evenings to communicate important revision information. For example, during Year 11 parents' evenings, give all students and parents Revision Menus with activities they can complete at home for all the topics they need to revise. This gives parents a clear and explicit idea of what their child can do at home, as opposed to just reading their notes.
- Use the school's newsletter to communicate important revision information.
- Provide parents with a regular revision newsletter.
- Outstanding departments offer 'revise with your child' sessions. Use these to demonstrate effective, subject-specific revision activities to students who attend with their parents.

Taking it further

If your school employs a learning mentor, use them! They can provide an essential communication point between parents and school and can be a vital conduit for more bespoke revision information for individual parental concerns.

Bonus idea

At the beginning of the year, provide parents and carers with a list of recommended revision resources, such as revision guides, websites, apps and books, for each subject. Giving parents this information so early not only helps them to prepare and keeps them informed but also helps tackle the tricky problem of budgeting for such resources.

#RevSupPar

Using examiners' reports

Getting it straight from the horse's mouth!

Examiners' reports are the main form of feedback from those who write the examinations our students sit. This should inform any kind of exam preparation within a revision programme.

After each exam, the examiners produce a report about the strengths and weaknesses of the candidates for each question within the exam, providing detailed and extremely useful information about the required skills for success. This feedback should be an integral part of preparing your students for the examination process.

An effective way to use the information is in the debriefing period of a mock examination. Use the examiners' reports to identify weaknesses within the mock examination performance. This can then guide students to tailor their revision so that it addresses these specific weaknesses, allowing them to make significant gains in the 'real thing'.

When conducting a debriefing session after a mock examination, provide a summary for each question of the advice given within the examiners' report to your students based on their performance. Below is a worked example of feedback for a question in a history exam.

Question 3 – Source Utility – 8 marks 'Those who attained marks in Band 3 or 4 of the mark scheme were able to make appropriate selections of words and phrases from the chosen source text and make references to the nature, origin and purpose considering the audience of the source.'

Teacher feedback based on examiners' reports The key to the top band answers is applying your knowledge gained from the

#Revisionreports

nature, origin and purpose of the source. Who wrote the source? Why did they write it? What is the relation of the source to the event? These are all valid questions to ask yourself, but you can also consider the stance and tone of the source and why they are approaching their subject in this way. Think about the audience the source is intended for too.

Key Mistake 'Students whose marks resided in Band 2 attempted to select and compare but often resorted to describing content and purpose, speculating on audience or making generalised comments about sentence length. These students often identified features such as tone, facts and bias, but then offered only generalised comments that, for example, they "disliked the suffragettes".'

Therefore the real value of examiners' reports in an effective revision programme is to direct students on what they need to improve and focus on in their revision and guide them on how to achieve maximum performance.

Taking it further

Exam boards often produce support materials in addition to exam reports that are well worth consulting. They include online discussions and can contain great advice and insights, which you can use in lessons.

Displays for revision

Revision is on show everywhere!

Displays are a ubiquitous feature of any school but how often are they under used or, worse still, ignored? An effective and interactive revision programme makes use of every resource to hand — and that includes displays.

#Revisiondisplay

The key purpose of classroom displays is to support the learning of students and stimulate interest in your subject. Some of the best examples of displays that support learning and revision are:

- **A question board** This is a blank display with the title 'Question Board' on which students are encouraged to post questions. You need a ready supply of post-it notes for students to write on. After agreeing on the topic to be revised, give students some DIRT to assess the gaps in their knowledge or skills that they want to improve. They post the question they want answered on the Question Board. Refer to the board throughout the session, ensuring that you cover all the points that students feel less confident about.
- **Model answers on display** This idea tackles what an A grade response looks like and gives an explanation of why it got the top grade.
- **Sentence starters** Students often find it hard to frame their answers to the exam criteria. They have the knowledge but not the technique. Display a series of sentence starters that students can refer to when practising exam questions.
- **Exam mark schemes** Display the exam mark schemes in your classroom. For example, present mark schemes on pictures of ladders with students climbing them. Making the schemes visually striking helps students to remember the key features.

Last-minute revision sessions

It is never too late . . .

Intervention is a key word in schools at the moment and an effective revision programme can be an important part of a school's intervention provision for exam classes. Last-minute revision ensures that students are supported right up to the exam.

Last-minute revision sessions are often held to support our students when nerves are high. There are always going to be students who have left their revision to the last minute and who require our support.

Here are some ideas, many provided by Stella Cottrell, that you could include in last-minute revision sessions to calm your students.

- Focus upon gaining a topic overview and looking at the bigger picture. Encourage students to first look at the gist of a topic, and then help them to make better use of any of the detail that they can recall. Using timelines in history or piecing together plot synopses in English would be ideal.
- Identify three key pieces of information for a topic, then make a link between each one or order them, such as in chronological order. Write down one reason why each piece of information is significant. Repeat the process three times.
- Make a single word mnemonic and share it with others in the last-minute revision session.
- Take a page from a revision guide that summarises a key topic. Underline the key words. Write them out in a mind map using one image to summarise each word, or list the key words and repeat them out loud with their definitions.

Teaching tip

In these sessions always emphasise that you are just re-capping what they know already and that there is nothing new in terms of content. The key outcome you want from a last-minute revision session, in my view, is to support and boost the confidence of your students. There is no better way to achieve this than through positive reinforcement.

Taking it further

In my recent revision programme, one element that proved particularly effective was holding a breakfast revision club. Run clubs on the morning of the exam, and spend 40 minutes or so going over the key overviews of the examination topics. The aim is to get students 'warmed up' and in the mood for the exam, taking the edge off nerves and engaging with high-quality revision right up to the point of entering the exam hall.

#Lastminrevision

Collaborative revision

Part 2

All square!

Square your revision and it multiplies . . .

This brilliant collaborative revision activity was inspired by the work of Isabella Wallace and Leah Kirkman. It gets students sharing their ideas and talking about what they know.

The beauty of this activity is that students do all the work and share their knowledge while you can sit back and watch. All you need is a blank sheet of A4 paper for each student. First, ask the students to fold their paper into eight equal squares – according to Wallace and Kirkman it should be like a perfect bar of chocolate. Nominate a topic and ask students to mentally recall everything they know about it in one-minute. Once they are prepared, students should circulate around the classroom and find out eight different things about the topic from eight different classmates. Each time students learn a new piece of information, they write it down in a square on their piece of paper to show they have understood what has been shared.

Once all students have collected eight pieces of information, hold a whole-class discussion. Sharing information further increases the students' knowledge bank for the topic, and can also reveal misconceptions, which can be corrected.

This is a great way to review and revise topics in a collaborative way without students relying on you to spoon-feed them the information they need. The activity is inclusive; even students who are stuck at the beginning can share the ideas they gather during the activity, and you will find that students who are confident about the topic often discover a nugget of information that they had forgotten.

#ALLSquare

Dominoes

Knock knock!

Dominoes is not just a game played by old men in a quiet pub. It can provide some serious revision fun and make for a quick-fire game of knowledge and wits.

This activity requires a little preparation on your part. You need a set of cards of around A6 size, each divided in half like a domino tile – there should be one for each student. You can use the table tool in Word to prepare the dominos. Each domino should have a question on one half and an answer on the other half but which do not match. These are reusable revision resources and you can give electronic copies to your students for them to print off and use outside the classroom.

Once you have prepared a set of dominoes, initiate a game with the whole class by giving one domino to each student. Any student can begin the activity by reading out the question on their domino. The student who believes that they have the answer on their domino reads it out – if the answer is correct, that student then reads out their question and the activity continues. If not, the search continues for the correct answer. When students have played their domino, they remain involved by discussing the answers given in the rest of the sequence.

This activity is a whole-class activity and it can be applied and differentiated in a variety of ways. Students can begin by playing in groups and once they're more confident they can make their own. The sets can be swapped with other groups within the class, promoting collaboration. As a whole-class activity, give the more able students two cards, so they have more information to look out for.

Teaching tip

Preparing for this activity is potentially time consuming, so only make a couple of sets. Once the students know how the activity works, get them to make their own sets. Ask them to give you an electronic copy so that you can check they are correct and use them with succeeding revision groups.

Taking it further

As a whole-class activity, add challenge by playing under timed conditions, with students taking it in turns to time how quickly the class can correctly go through all the answers. This reinforces students' knowledge and requires them to use key exam skills such as recalling under timed pressure.

#Domino

Find someone . . .

Tell me . . .

This collaborative whole-class activity encourages students to use each other as a revision resource.

For a class of around 30 students, you need to prepare between 9 and 15 questions or tasks. Arrange these in a grid, leaving room for students to write the answer as well as the name of the student who provided the answer. Each student will need a copy of this find-someone grid.

Include a mix of knowledge-based questions and application-of-knowledge tasks, with varying degrees of difficulty. By doing this, you automatically build differentiation for all abilities and learning styles. The following examples are for content on the rise of Hitler. Find someone who . . .

- knows when the Munich Beer Hall Putsch took place;
- can name one of Hitler's henchmen during the 1920s;
- can explain how Germany dealt with the crises of 1923;
- can sketch a diagram showing how the Weimar Republic tried to deal with the Great Depression.

Each student seeks someone who can answer a question or perform a task on his or her grid. This person then writes down the answer and the name of the person in the corresponding box in their grid. The activity finishes when all the boxes are filled in.

Follow up with a class discussion. Encourage tasks with a degree of performance, such as a jingle, rap or drawing, to be shared with the whole class.

The lift test

Going up?

This quick-fire verbal presentation activity helps students to consider specific issues and present their ideas to a fixed deadline.

The lift test gets students to consider the core importance of a specific argument, and the central pieces of evidence to support a specific point. Start by giving each student, pair or group a scenario, such as:

- You have written a book about *To Kill a Mockingbird* in relation to the Civil Rights Movement in 1960s America.
- You have produced a documentary called *Henry VIII – Hero or Tyrant?*
- You have written an article on the significance of bees.
- You have created a public art project about the three most influential modern artists.

The student has been granted five minutes to present their pitch, but when they arrive for the appointment they are told 'Sorry, something has come up, give me an overview on the way to my car'. The student now has one minute to pitch their argument in the lift down to the car park.

This is extremely effective as it forces the students to give an overview of a specific issue or argument that they may face in the exam. It is flexible and can be modified for any subject, requires very little preparation on your part, and gets students to practise exam skills such as:

- communicating an important argument concisely;
- evaluating the main points of an argument;
- considering the significance of the evidence that supports the key points and emphasising the 'selling point';
- presenting the knowledge in a structured manner.

Teaching tip

To get all students actively involved at all times, set specific tasks or questions for them to complete while they watch the presentations, and give some students responsibilities such as timing the presentations or writing the key points on the board. This avoids passive participation and boredom.

Taking it further

Set groups of students contrasting arguments and then ask them to present their lift test consecutively. The audience must consider how the same information is presented differently to persuade them of alternative arguments, as well as judging if the key points included in the presentation are the most significant. Are there alternative points that are more important?

#Lifttest

Magpie cards

When in doubt – steal!

Stealing thoughts and ideas is part of a healthy collaborative process!

Revision can be isolating, with its traditional image of students chained to desks, learning large chunks of information that they can regurgitate in an exam. Challenge this perception by encouraging students to share ideas and revision tips.

'Magpie cards' encourage sharing in the classroom in a light-hearted yet effective manner. Give students a card each with a magpie on and give them permission to go around the classroom and talk with other students, exchanging ideas and information. This can be used in revision sessions in a number of contexts:

- For students who are struggling with a revision task they can use it when they need additional help. To monitor this, the selected student has to report to you (or a TA) what they found when they used the card. This not only promotes collaboration but also gives you an in-built progress check.
- Give a 'magpie card' to every student, then at a chosen point in the revision session, call out 'magpie!'. Students must then share one piece of information that they have found out from their revision with up to three other students. Students must then use the information exchanged within the revision task being completed.
- For revision group work, give each group one 'magpie card'. At a given point one member of each group takes the card and acts as an envoy by trading information with other groups.

#Magpiecards

Pecha-Kucha

20 x 20 presentation = 20:20 [re]vision.

Pecha-Kucha is a great format for presentations. It tests student knowledge and ensures that they get to the heart of their revision topics.

Pecha-Kucha, or 'chatter', is a format of presentations that was established by Astrid Klein and Mark Dytham, two Australian architects who were bored by flabby PowerPoint presentations. Pecha-Kucha aims to keep presentations tight and focused by using the following rules:

- Students create a set of visual slides. There are 20 images, which must been shown for 20 seconds each – the presentation must be timed.
- The presentation must last 6 minutes and 40 seconds, and the slides must play automatically. The presentation must match the slide being shown, and when the slides run out, the presentation is over.

This is an excellent challenge for A Level students. Overviews of topics or themes make the best content for a Pecha-Kucha exercise. They encourage students to think about the bigger picture – which they need to do if the exam includes synoptic questions – and think carefully about what to include. Students will need to decide what is important enough to include. This can be a hook for discussion after each presentation – get the audience to look for what has been left out and ask the presenters to justify their choices.

Build up a library of the slides so that you have valuable revision resources for a variety of topics.

Teaching tip

It is well worth moving away from PowerPoint presentations and asking students to explore other digital presentation packages. Prezi and Haiku Deck are particularly suited for this kind of activity as these packages are better geared for visual presentations and steer students away from the temptation to add text.

Taking it further

Why not try other presentation structures used by industry? They can be a challenging, real-life framework for students to work within and, therefore, prepare students' skills for the work place as well as revising. Look at Ignite and Lightning Talk presentation frameworks and, if you are particularly ambitious, Speed Geeking, as a starting point.

#PechaKucha

Peer assessment

What the child can do in collaboration today, he or she can do alone tomorrow.

Since the work of Wiliam and Black, peer assessment has become an important strand in the Assessment for Learning toolkit can enhance student understanding and relieve the pressure on you!

Teaching tip

As a follow-up have in place a feed-forward/ improvement task that students complete immediately afterwards to show that they have made progress from it. This emphasises the importance of peer assessment and embeds the feedback students have received from their peers.

Active revision must include opportunities for collaboration and discussion, and many peer-assessment activities can help you achieve this. The key to ensuring these activities are a success is to dissuade students from just marking 'Well done!' or 'Could do better,' on each other's work. Encourage collaboration and application of knowledge of course content and exam skills, and demand explanation of judgements.

Revision partners Randomly generate pairs and change them regularly. Set specific tasks, such as swapping work midway through an activity and completing each other's work.

Celebration student Give a student, or a pair of students, a target to look out for in a revision lesson. This could be 'effective use of sentence starters' or 'quality explanation of a relevant point in an exam question'. At the end of the lesson, the Celebration student highlights two students who have hit the given target and when they did it. Allow the Celebration student five minutes during the lesson to move around the classroom looking for students who have hit the target.

Anonymous models Use examples of work from anonymous students. Allow students to read them and put post-it notes with What Went Well (WWW) and EBI (Even Better If) comments. Use this and the relevant mark schemes as a focus for a class discussion to compare and contrast viewpoints on the work.

Bonus idea ★

Peer-generated questions Generate a set of questions from the students, then let the students themselves answer them and share their responses, either in groups or in a class discussion. Try using an honesty box, where students can write a revision question on a post-it note and place it in the box, or ask students to work in groups to create five revision questions which summarise a topic.

#Peerrevision

Peer mentoring

Peer mentoring – an approach in which one child instructs another child in material on which the first is an expert and the second is a novice.

Peer mentoring is not a new concept; it was encouraged by philosopher Baltasar Gracian in the 17th century. Using it as part of a revision programme expands your expert network and varies the input so it does not rely upon you all the time.

Recent research shows that a planned and coherent peer-mentoring programme can bring great benefits to learning, such as increased motivation and enhanced understanding – for both the mentee and mentor. Drawing on the experiences of students who have recently sat the exam to help your current students can be incredibly useful. A few ideas for how to use peer mentoring:

- At the end of a revision programme, ask your students to come up with one revision tip that they have found particularly useful. Collate them, type them up on one sheet, and use them at the beginning of the revision programme with your class for the following year.
- Set up a mentoring scheme where A2 students mentor AS students, on a voluntary basis. The AS students benefit from the input of someone who has recently sat the exam and receive advice on helpful wider reading . It benefits the A2 students by enabling them to keep their knowledge and skills fresh, and deepens their grasp of the subject.
- Invite A2 students to make a directed and active contribution to your lessons, such as giving a short presentation on a topic area or on the skills needed for success. Peer mentoring can be especially useful for practical subjects, such as maths and economics, where a student might benefit from support with applications and calculations.

Taking it further

Peer mentoring can be a whole-school focus. It is clear that students benefit greatly from learning from each other, not just in terms of progress but also in terms of strengthening the school ethos and community. Putting some training in place for students who mentor is crucial for it to be meaningful and effective. The resources from the University of the First Age are incredibly useful in training students with their programme Leading Other Learners offering a wealth of training materials.

Bonus idea ★

Why not ask GCSE, AS or A2 students to lead assemblies which have a revision theme?

#Peermenrev

Perform it!

The smell of the greasepaint! The roar of the crowd!

Examinations are all about showing and applying your knowledge in a variety of ways. Why not allow students to show off their knowledge by performing it.

It can be challenging to set up activities and learning experiences which allow students to explain their learning and deploy skills such as analysis, explanation and evaluation. Using performing-arts techniques can be very memorable for students and have that 'stickability' factor – essential for any successful revision session. Here are some performing-arts revision activities.

Freeze frame In groups, students select the most significant learning point in a text, experiment, sporting activity, historical event or scene from a novel and provide a tableau explaining that learning point. The audience must decipher the meaning and suggest how each student is contributing to it.

A sports commentary Ask students to summarise a topic in the style of a sports commentary. Encourage them to think carefully about what type of commentary would be suitable for the content to be revised. For example, would a commentary for a race or for a team game be more appropriate.

A speech in the style of . . . Students present their learning as a speech in a given style. Do this randomly, by writing down different styles on pieces of paper and asking students to draw them out of a hat. Examples of styles are:

- a prime minister
- a television presenter
- the headteacher (for the really brave!).

Mixing revision content with a specific style not only promotes creativity but also asks the students to think more carefully about language and presentation, sharpening skills in analysis, explanation and evaluation.

Create song lyrics This activity requires students to experiment with content and vocabulary by substituting their own words into songs to summarise a topic to be revised. You can give students a free choice (which can be risky!) or provide a choice of song titles or music from well-known television shows.

Draw it! Give students a large piece of paper and ask them to summarise a key learning point in just one picture – using no words. You can extend this by grouping students in small teams and assigning them a different part of a topic to draw. Together, these parts constitute a whole, such as a scientific process, stages of a movement in sport or dance, or a chapter from a novel. Put together, the drawings summarise an entire topic. Students should be encouraged to assess each other's pictures, thinking about what has been included and left out. To debrief, get students to use the images to write a summary paragraph of the whole topic.

Sell it! This activity can be done in pairs, groups or as a class. Give each student an aspect from the content you are revising. This could be a character, viewpoint, idea, symbol or a cause of an event. With limited preparation time, each student has to 'sell' their aspect within 60 seconds. Encourage students to summarise the unique selling point of the factor they have been given in a catchy tagline. For variety give the more able an obscure factor to sell and the less able a more straightforward aspect. This is a great activity to make students consider the significance of different aspects of the content they need to revise.

#Performit

Collaborative revision placemats

Sharing is caring.

This engaging idea from Gael Luzet gets students sharing, recording and then summarising ideas and is ideal for revision.

Taking it further

Placemats can make great visual revision aids and can be pinned up on the classroom wall towards the end of the revision session. Students can then look at other groups' work and note down ideas, points or facts which they had previously forgotten as the final stage of the revision session.

This collaborative activity is a great alternative to brainstorming and can be easily harnessed for revision purposes. Students should work in groups of four, each with a placemat like the one below, ideally in A1, A2 or A3 size.

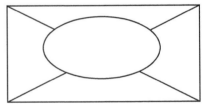

Students should be seated on each side of the placemat with an outer space to themselves. The activity works in two stages.

Stage 1 Each student records their ideas, responses, views or facts on a given topic in their outer section.

Stage 2 Students then write an agreed response in the central oval.

This can be used in a variety of contexts:

- Give each group an exam question and ask them to use the placemat to collaborate ideas to come up with the key points.
- Give each member an area to brainstorm and record what they know, then summarise the entire topic in the oval.
- Use this task to brainstorm a topic that was taught some time ago, encouraging students to recall knowledge, and share ideas.

#Revisionplacemats

Revision tree

Branch out and explore your learning . . .

This collaborative revision activity can help you sum up a topic and organise its content in a very short space of time – great for helping students to remember chunks of information.

Creating a revision tree requires very little preparation on your part. All you need is a stack of post-it notes and a picture of an outline of a tree that you can project onto a board (or you can just draw one on the board). On each branch write a sub-category of the topic. For example:

- causes, events and consequences of a specific event;
- the different stages of an experiment;
- chapters in a novel;
- life of a key artist, writer or scientist;
- vocabulary for a topic such as holidays and shopping.

It also works for structuring an exam response, with each branch representing different paragraphs of an essay or the sequence of thinking through a problem.

Once you have presented your revision tree, divide the class into groups. Each group is responsible for a different branch within the tree. In groups, students will write relevant ideas, evidence, information or content on their post-it notes. They will then stick their post-it notes onto the relevant branch of the tree. Using the completed tree as a prompt, go through each branch with the class, ensuring that the information of the post-it notes is relevant, and ask the class if anything else needs to be added. Once this has been completed, you have a revision tree that summarises and organises the selected topic that students can make notes from.

Teaching tip

To make a permanent record of this revision aid, take photographs of the completed revision tree and post them on the VLE or school intranet system for students to access at all times.

Taking it further

Create a worksheet with a blank revision tree outline on it. Students can then create their own revision trees as part of their revision programme at home. In lessons you could ask them to nominate a topic to be revised, fill in the sub-categories for each branch, then swap with a revision partner to fill in the information, facts and ideas for each sub-category.

#Revisiontree

Revision triads

The secret society of revision . . .

Revision triads help you create an in-built, peer assisted support network without any extra monitoring on the teacher's part.

Taking it further

When using this strategy, you may want to tap into individual strengths of the group more deeply by assigning specific tasks for group members. They could be given a list of such tasks to choose from. For example, an individual may be responsible for checking the revision notes within the group to see if they are completed, and another may be responsible for creating specific revision resources.

Learning triads make an effective support strategy, and can be easily transferred to create revision triads. These involve dividing your teaching group into smaller groups of three students —either by friendships or ability. Each student in a triad is responsible for supporting the learning and revision of the other two.

Group members of the triad should ensure that:

- they share revision materials and ideas;
- they work together in revision lessons;
- each group member is pulling their weight, revising and sharing materials equally;
- each group member is up-to-date with revision notes;
- they make time to discuss any points they are unclear about from the lessons.

You can allow time for the triads to work together in lessons, whether during group work or when you give students time to check and complete a set of tasks such as sharing revision resources. Much of the work can happen outside the classroom, especially in the Sixth Form where you can encourage triads to spend non-contact time working together, sharing notes, ideas and resources.

Working in this way promotes collaboration and is excellent preparation for higher or further education, where students need to take responsibility for their own learning. Students are less reliant from you for their revision programme and they develop wider skills other than those needed to passing an exam.

#Revisiontriads

Runaround!

Can you beat the clock?

This active revision exercise is very much like the 1970s quiz show Runaround hosted by Mike Reid. It is inspired by the brilliant work of Paul Ginnis and requires speed and precision from all students.

Students work in teams, competing against each other to complete a set of questions. You need to prepare a set of questions (ten is a good number, each on a separate sheet). To make it easier, each set should be in a different colour. Each set should be placed on the teacher's table at the front of the classroom. You also have the option to give each group source material from which they can find the answers to their questions.

When you start, a nominated 'runner' from each group fetches the first question only from their set of questions and returns to their group. The group decide on their answer and write it down underneath the question, then the runner brings it to you to be marked. If it is correct then the runner takes the second question back to the group. If it is not correct, the question is returned for the group to try again. Writers and runners should rotate between questions. The first group to complete the questions correctly is the winner. Debrief the class by going through the answers and outlining the skills required to successfully complete the set of questions. Students can then write up their answers.

This is a great collaborative exercise and provides a high level of energy and gives students the opportunity to apply their knowledge under pressure. The activity can be used for any subject that has a written assessment, and for any topic.

Teaching tip

This revision activity requires some preparation to set up – formulating questions, photocopying, arranging question sets – and can be deceptively time consuming. To cut down on preparation time, use questions from exam papers and, for the more demanding extended writing questions, ask for an essay plan rather than a detailed response.

Taking it further

This activity can be adapted in many ways. One of the best ways is to group students in rough ability groups and give them separate questions, enabling the learning to be differentiated. Groups having different questions on separate areas of a topic can lead on to peer teaching.

#Runaround

Snowball

Link and you learn.

Linking knowledge together so that students can describe and explain their ideas is a crucial skill for examinations. This fun activity prompts students to think more deeply about content they need to revise in a collaborative and supportive framework.

Teaching tip

This activity can be challenging, at first, for some of the less able students. Provide visual clues, sentence starters and key words to support them.

Taking it further

If you are completing the activity in small groups, add challenge by providing a short list of key words that students have to include in their chain, crossing them off when they are used. Alternatively, add an element of 'Taboo' and provide a short list of key words that students cannot include – this may be more suitable for the more able group.

#Snowball

This activity can be used at the end of a revision session and can provide a quick and easy way to test students' knowledge and application of what they have learned, with no preparation.

The activity can be carried out as a class, or small groups can perform their snowball chain in front of the rest of the class, who can then challenge and discuss. To start, you make an initial short factual statement, such as 'The Second World War began in 1939', which is passed on to a student who is expected to add a linked fact to the initial statement, for example 'The Second World War began in 1939 and a key cause was Hitler's aggressive foreign policy'. The next student adds a third fact to the snowballing statement and so on.

You can monitor the outcome in a number of ways such as asking a reliable student to write the statements on the board to then review. Alternatively, you could allow students to challenge each other's additions. This is an effective element of the activity as it includes the whole class, encouraging them to listen to each other closely and remember and evaluate what is said.

To add a greater sense of competition, do it as a whole class and allow five seconds for each student to add their link. If correct the student remains standing; if not they have to sit down. Last student standing wins!

Getting students on TASC

This lesson's main TASC is . . .

Questioning and thinking frameworks help develop students' exam skills and are an important part of an effective revision programme. The TASC (Thinking Actively in a Social Context) wheel, created by Belle Wallace, is a brilliant framework to use.

The TASC wheel is an eight-part process designed to provide students with an excellent framework for working through a revision programme, either as a whole or topic by topic. It can also be applied when stuck in the middle of an exam paper. Training students through the TASC wheel helps to organise their thinking in a revision context. The stages and how they can be applied to a revision context are:

- **What do I know about this?** Students list everything they know about the topic to be revised.
- **What is the task?** Students consider how the topic is to be examined. What kind of questions could come up? What stimulus (e.g. diagrams, text, sources and photographs) might they have in the exam? The mark schemes are very important here for students to understand how they are going to be assessed.
- **How many ideas can I think of?** Students organise their knowledge into using tools such as mind maps, Carroll Diagrams and Comparison Alleys to help them.
- **Which is the best idea?** Students rank their ideas in order of significance or importance.
- **Let's do it!** Students complete the exam question/task they have been preparing for.
- **How well did I do?** Using the mark scheme, students peer assess each other's work.
- **Let's tell someone!** Students share their work with a revision partner or a revision triad.

Teaching tip

Graphic presentations of the TASC wheel are freely available with a quick internet search. Print one off to display in your classroom and constantly refer to it to help structure students' thinking and working patterns during the revision programme.

Taking it further

As an alternative to peer assessing each other's work, ask students to use the mark scheme to predict how well they have done. When you mark and return their work students can compare their prediction with the mark you gave them.

#Revisiontasc

Revision in lessons

Part 3

A to Z of revision

Know your topic all the way from A to Z.

This deceptively challenging, but easy to set up, activity takes students through a revision topic all the way from A to Z.

#A2Zrev

All you need for this activity is a blank sheet of paper for each student. Students can work individually, in pairs or in small teams for this task. Ask each student, pair or team to list each letter of the alphabet on a piece of paper and assign them a topic or section of content to revise. The students' task is to think of a word that is connected with the topic for each letter of the alphabet.

This simple activity can be differentiated in several ways and tailored to the abilities of a wide range of students:

- For the less able, leave out the more challenging letters, such as Q, X and Z.
- For the middle ability, allow a quota of descriptive words. For example, you could allow 'blame' for the Treaty of Versailles or 'clever' for Sherlock Holmes, but these words must be justified and explained.
- For the able students, ask for each word to be explained. Alternatively, choose five letters at random for which the students have to think of two more words.
- Set a time limit, depending on how much depth you want students to go into the task and what time you want to devote to it in your lesson.
- Conduct a class discussion afterwards in which students have to justify their choice of word. Class members are allowed to challenge the justification even use a random name generator, such as those found at tripticoplus.com to choose which student presents their work.

Get out the bunting

What are we celebrating, Miss?

Progress and effective revision is always worth celebrating. Why not do so by making and putting up some bunting?

Putting up bunting is one way of celebrating an important event, and effective learning should always be an important event in your classroom, so why not celebrate it with this technique?

Give each student a piece of card printed with a triangle outline which will be the students' contribution to the class bunting. Give each student an area to revise, and then ask them to make links to separate content so that every area of the chosen topic is covered. Students must choose the most interesting or important ideas or facts about their area and present these in any way they like on their triangle. This allows for students of all abilities to choose how to present their revision and the activity can then be easily personalised. For example, you could ask the more able to produce a double sided pennant, or challenge a student of a middle ability to limit the number of words they use on their bunting.

The outcome is a series of triangles that summarise a wide range of content, which you can attach to string and put up around your classroom as an effective and distinctive display which can be referred to in subsequent lessons.

Allowing students to choose how they are going to show their revision promotes independence and allows them to be creative by applying their knowledge differently. These are important revision skills and give students a permanent reminder of their revision.

> **Bonus idea** ★
>
> Bunting can be used to display different stages or developments in a topic, such as a timeline for the Cold War, the different stages of a novel in chronological order, or the processes of an experiment.

#Bunting

Chunk it!

Break your revision down into tasty morsels.

Chunking helps students to handle large tracts of information with confidence and enables them to improve their memory skills.

Teaching tip

Use 'Chunking Triangles' as a way of summarising learning in revision sessions. Students can complete them while they are making notes or use completed 'Chunking Triangles' as a sequence of headings to structure their notes. By visually mapping the structure of a topic students can also revisit this time and time again.

Chunking information stems from the work of Nobel Prize winner, Herbert Simon whose studies argued that the human brain can hold up to five 'chunks' of information in its short-term memory. The chunk of information can vary significantly in size – from a single word, number or phrase to a whole story. Therefore, breaking down large tracts of information into chunks can assist the memory in holding information as well as providing a framework for organising information when revising.

One of the most effective frameworks is the 'Chunking Triangle', created by Stephen Bowkett. Here's an example:

Taking it further

Give students incomplete 'Chunking Triangles' to fill in. This can promote excellent discussions about what information best fits the gaps you have left. Alternatively, reverse it and consider what information deserves to be left out. Encourage explanation and justification – a great way to promote and practise important exam skills.

At the tip is the largest chunk of information, a theme, topic heading or issue which can be broken down into smaller pieces as you work your way to the top edge of the triangle. Links are also made between the chunks within the layers. This method taps into the natural workings of the short-term memory, as well as encouraging deep learning of information.

#Chunkit

Continuums

Fill the vacuum of knowledge with a continuum!

Continuums are perhaps the most popular form of graphic organisers of knowledge and should be an essential addition to any teacher's revision toolkit.

Continuums are an excellent tool for organising judgements in an efficient way. Being visual they are also a powerful revision aid. There are a number of practical applications to help with revision, which vary in the amount of preparation time required. Here are some effective methods.

- Give the students an exam question requiring an extended written response that includes several factors. Type these factors onto cards that the students can cut out and ask them to place the factors on a single line continuum, with one end being 'significant' and the other 'less significant'. Students then need to write a short paragraph on each explaining why they have placed it on the continuum where they have. This is great preparation for writing essays, as it requires not only organisation of information but also skills in explanation and application of knowledge.

- A more physical approach is to clear the desks and lay a line (using a rope, masking tape or chalk) in the centre of the room. This is your continuum. Position opposing views at either end. Allow your students to consider their view before standing on the continuum where they think their view fits. Ask chosen students to justify their view and then discuss with the other students if the view is in the correct place on the continuum. This develops collaboration, thinking on your feet and justifying a viewpoint.

Bonus idea ★

This method is good for organising factual information, such as events, dates and characters. Get your students to stand in a line – this can act as a continuum. Define what each end represents. Give each student a piece of information on a card which they must keep to themselves. Now they need to organise themselves in the correct order, for example in chronological order. However, they must first do this in silence. At the end of the activity, initiate a whole class debrief and ask students to share the details of their card.

#Continuum

Create your own exam paper

Test yourself with your own exam paper!

To really get to know an exam paper, you have to create one, so why not make your own exam papers . . .

Ensuring that your students interact with the exam papers they will be sitting is an essential part of any revision programme. Ensuring that they know every component of the exam paper is critical for success, but this can be challenging to make engaging and attention grabbing. One way that this can be done in a fully interactive manner is to allow students to create their own exam paper based on the key components of the exam they will face. You will need to give them the following information.

- The question stems for each question in each section of the exam paper.
- The marks that each question is worth.
- Any stimuli that the students will have in the exam paper (maps and graphs in geography, a text in English, sources in history, diagrams in Science) which questions will be based around.
- Key instructions of what questions to tackle and how many questions will be available to choose from.
- Mark schemes.

Of course, students are aware of all this information beforehand but, in my experience, many students overlook this despite being given the information early on in the exam course and constantly using it when answering questions or receiving feedback which is based around the exam criteria.

#Exampaper

Defend it!

The case for the defence, Your Honour, is . . .

This activity, from Mike Gershon, ensures that students apply and present their knowledge in a format ideal for exam preparation.

Honing your students' skills in applying knowledge to create an argument is an important part of preparing them for the exams. All you need for this activity are a number of linked interpretations or statements related to a common topic. For example, if you were revising 1920s prosperity in America you might have statements such as:

- mass production was the most important factor in explaining prosperity in America during the 1920s;
- most people enjoyed a better standard of living in America during the 1920s;
- prohibition's most important impact was the growth of organised crime;
- the radio was the most important consumer good developed during the 1920s in America.

Give students, in pairs or groups, one of the statements from the list. They have to prepare an argument that supports their statement. Remind them of what to think about when making their argument, for example, what examples from your own knowledge can you give to support the statement? What language do you need to be more persuasive in the presentation of your argument?

Once the arguments have been completed, each group or pair presents their defence. Next, the class is invited to challenge it. The presenters can rebut the challenge. Once everyone has presented, ask the class to vote for the most accurate and persuasive statement. This can be presented as a continuum, with 'strong ' at one end and 'weak' at the other.

Teaching tip

To support your students with the demands of language, use a learning mat with words and sentence starters on it to help students construct a persuasive piece of writing. These are readily available online and can be modified for your own needs or used as a model for inspiration to create your own.

Taking it further

You can easily flip this activity by asking students to attack the statement rather than defend it, while the audience tries to ask questions in defence of the statement. This requires subtly different skills and is ideal to stretch and challenge students who aspire to the higher grades.

#Defendit

Fill my brain

How much do you need? How much can you fit in?

Cramming is a well-known feature of revising – however it is not the most brain friendly way of learning. This fun activity encourages students to cram their brains with as much information as they can handle.

'Fill my brain' is one of my favourite activities for getting students to summarise their learning. The basic idea is to ask students to draw the outline of their brain, and then fill it with everything they have learned in the revision lesson. They can use key words, bullet points, drawings, or anything else they like. Once this has been completed you can ask the students to highlight the most important point all the new points that have yet to be revised.

This simple task requires very little preparation, and can also be applied in other ways.

- Students work in pairs for this variation. Each student draws a brain and fills it in with their knowledge of the topic to be revised. Give them a time limit, which is deliberately not enough time to fill the brain completely. Once the time is up, ask students to swap brains with their partner, who then fills in the gaps with their own knowledge.
- This variation requires a tiny bit of preparation. List five key words from a topic. Ask students to fill in their brains, with the catch: either that they can't use the key words or that they have to use all five golden words. Then discuss why these words are important, and talk about possible alternative words.
- 'Fill my brain' can easily be completed in groups, using marker pens and sugar paper to summarise a topic and then present it to the rest of the class.

#Fillmybrain

Five lists in five minutes

There is nothing like a list to help you get organised!

This competitive revision activity helps students to organise, share and list their knowledge in timed conditions.

'Five lists in five minutes', created by the University of the First Age, is a paired or group activity and allows students to work both collaboratively and competitively. It works best as either a warm-up exercise to get students thinking or as a plenary to summarise the session. Either way, it promotes sharing knowledge as well as adding a competitive and fun atmosphere to the revision session.

Each group of students is provided with a sheet specifying five categories for which they must list their knowledge. These categories can be linked under a common theme. For example, five lists for a common topic in a Government and Politics revision session could be:

- examples of insider pressure groups . . .
- arguments for referendums . . .
- roles of the civil service . . .
- arguments against EU membership . . .
- outcomes of the 2015 General Election . . .

The class is challenged to complete the five lists in pairs or groups, as fully as possible in five minutes. It is advisable to place a limit of ten items per list so that students do not get too carried away and focus on only one or two lists.

After five minutes, the groups then present their lists. To give it an extra competitive edge, points could be awarded for each item of knowledge on the list, with one point awarded for each item of relevant knowledge and two for each item that no other group or pair has included.

Teaching tip

This activity is sufficiently flexible to allow differentiation by placing different limitations on the lists – some may require five items of knowledge while other, more difficult lists, may require ten.

Taking it further

Once students are used to this activity, ask them to come up with their own five lists and test each other. This adds to student engagement and enables students to direct their own revision.

Bonus idea ★

The lists can be shaped to resemble exam questions, and students can compare the lists to the relevant mark scheme. With this twist, you are not only revising knowledge but also encouraging students to apply their knowledge to the mark schemes.

#5in5

Flip it!

Oh flipping heck sir!

This card game sharpens the memory, and can be played anywhere.

This simple memory technique came from Bill McClaren, the rugby union commentator, who used it to remember players' names and jersey numbers. It can be easily adapted to help with revision.

Give students an A4 sheet of card with a blank grid of 16 small rectangles, which they can cut out themselves. On one side of each card, students write a question that requires a short answer. On the reverse side, they write the answer. Once this has been completed, students lay the cards out in front of them, question side up. They answer each question, and turn the card over. If the answer is correct, they leave the card answer side up, if incorrect they leave it question side up and return to it once all the questions have been attempted.

To add challenge, ask students to answer the questions in a set time, or see which student can complete their questions in the fastest time.

This has many applications, such as:

- maths – symbols
- MFL – vocabulary
- history – key dates and events
- English – characters
- art – genres and styles

This activity gives students a handy and flexible revision aid that can be used at any time, it trains the memory to retain and recall information, it can be used for almost every subject, and it allows students to be more independent.

#Flipit

How to . . .

I know how to do this now, sir, it's just when and where!

Once you have set this activity up you may never need an instruction manual or revision guide again.

This activity requires students to make a 'How to' booklet. If you are focusing on knowledge, and I would in the first instance, this can be applied to practically any topic for any subject. Some effective examples include:

- how to order food in German
- how to tackle probability questions in maths
- how to make an attractive bird table.

The activity requires the student to think carefully about the processes and stages of tasks needed for successful completion. The booklet should be short, sharp and have a clearly defined limit of pages and words. This sharpens student focus and they have to edit, thinking more carefully about what to include in their booklet. You should direct students to include a variety of pictures, diagrams and words – so they are able to present their knowledge in different ways.

Another spin is to ask students to prepare booklets that specifically focus upon different types of questions in the exam, such as:

- how to tackle source reliability questions in history;
- how to tackle French listening examinations;
- how to tackle the practical PE exam.

For this, students need to use model answers, exam mark schemes and text books. Thus students would increase their understanding of these important documents, as well as creating a valuable revision aid. The 'How to' booklet can then be used by the rest of the class.

Teaching tip

The weaker students may struggle to produce a 'How to' booklet independently, so have some extra resources to hand, such as an exemplar booklet, key words, sentence starters, simplified exam mark schemes, visual clues and hooks and model exam answers, to get them started.

Taking it further

A long term strategy could be to collect as many student-designed 'How to' booklets as possible and create a department-based library for students in succeeding years. To promote the profile of the activity and your value of the booklets, you could give the best ones the highest available reward, such as a headteacher's commendation. This will also show parents how well their child is revising and making progress.

#Howto

Grenade questions

That lesson went with a bang!

It is always good to make students think, apply their knowledge and make links. Throwing in a grenade question will help students do this and improve the quality of their explanations.

Teaching tip

These grenade question stems are great to summarise learning at the end of a lesson but can also make for an effective homework assignment, – students can prepare an answer at home and then share in a class discussion at the beginning of the following lesson.

Asking students rigorous, yet engaging, questions to improve their thinking skills and to apply their knowledge to prompt discussion and debate can be tricky. Here are a few open-ended question stems that can be used in a revision session to promote discussion, thinking and to make links within topics.

Without or without you

The question stem is 'Without . . .there would be no . . .'

Some applications of this question stem in a revision session could be:

- Without Buddha there would be no . . .
- Without Mr. Birling there would be no . . .

This question stem encourages students to consider consequences, connections, and think laterally.

Would you rather be?

The question stem is 'Would you rather be . . .or . . .?'

Some applications could be:

- Would you rather be an equilateral or isosceles triangle?
- Would you rather be Berlin or Paris?

This question stem encourages students to make comparisons and links between two factors or items and explain judgements.

The thing most valuable to you

The question stem is 'What is the most valuable thing to . . .?'

Some applications could be:

- What is the most valuable thing to a Sikh?
- What is the most valuable thing to Pablo Picasso?

This question stem encourages students to think empathetically as well as to think about the significance of related factors and information.

For better or worse

The question stem is 'Is it better or worse . . .?'

Some applications could be:

- Is it better or worse that computers exist?
- Is it better or worse that Richard Nixon resigned rather than face trial?

This question stem promotes discussion, as well as encouraging students to consider different viewpoints on the same issue.

Significance

The question stem is 'Who/what is the most significant . . . or . . .?'

Some applications could be:

- Who is the most significant - Sherlock Holmes or Dr Watson?
- What is the most significant - the Berlin Wall or Sputnik?

This question stem promotes prioritising, comparison, contrasting and explanation.

Who would win in a fight . . .

The question stem is 'Who would win in a fight . . .or . . .?'

Some applications could be:

- Who would win in a fight a volcano or a tsunami?
- Who would win in a fight a rat or a flea?

This question stem encourages imaginative comparison and can provoke lively discussion.

Taking it further

To add fun to this, set the question stem and pick out a card from your revision card games pack to decide upon the factor or factors to be included in the question.

#Grenadeq

Watch that iceberg!

Make sure you identify an iceberg question before your exam answer sinks like the Titanic!

Icebergs can be dangerous, as the Titanic sadly found out. Iceberg questions can be equally dangerous to success in exams.

Teaching tip

Have extra iceberg outline diagrams to hand so that students can take them away and use them for planning answers.

Some exam questions are straightforward, while others, particularly those that demand a longer written response, are more tricky and have a 'hidden agenda' that may not be immediately apparent .

Iceberg questions were first defined by Dale Banham, a humanities adviser and prolific exam text book writer for history. This type of question usually requires a degree of explanation, analysis and evaluation in order to reach the higher levels, and tends to use such question stems as:

- How far . . .?
- How important was . . .?
- What was the significance of . . .?

Taking it further

Iceberg questions make a striking wall display, with worked examples and an explanation of what they are and how to identify them. Having this on constant display in your classroom gives your students a reference point when tackling such questions, and something for you to refer to when explaining what iceberg questions are and how they work.

An effective way of training students to handle these questions is to use a diagram of an iceberg to organise relevant information. In simplistic terms, one quarter of an iceberg is above the water while three quarters of it is beneath the water. Using a diagram, students write what they know about the issue raised in the question in the part above the water. Next they fill in the 'unseen' part of the iceberg with linked factors and information that provide the counterargument to the one in the question. This is the 'hidden agenda'.

Using an iceberg diagram and using it to plan answers adds a level of sophistication to essay planning, allowing students to recognise questions that have a 'hidden agenda' as well as enabling them to reach the higher level skill set.

#Iceberg

Learning grids for revision

Can you link box 4 with box 10?

Learning grids will help students to link their learning and explain their ideas in a variety of contexts.

Learning grids are grids of 12 numbered squares. In each square there is a word or image connected to a topic or a sub-topic. Either give the grid to the students on a piece of paper or, project it onto an interactive white board. In pairs, students roll a 12-sided die twice. They must locate the corresponding boxes on the grid from their two rolls of the die and find a way to link the two images or words together.

For example, using the prohibition board example from the online resources, if a student rolled a 3 – the picture is of a speakeasy – and a 7 – which is a bootlegger – the student would have to write down a link between the two. Here, the students have to apply their knowledge, this encourages them to use subject-specific vocabulary as well as thinking more deeply about the topic.

Learning grids promote curiosity. You can add to this by introducing a 12-sided die. When you hand out these unusual dice, you will hook the students because they are being able to use different equipment. Such dice are available online and in gaming shops.

Learning grids promote challenge. Some links caused by the random nature of the dice can be extremely difficult and students have to think laterally to make an effective link. However, the real value of these resources is encourage students to work collaboratively and discuss their learning while revising any topic for any subject.

> **Teaching tip**
>
> This activity can be easily differentiated. You can ask the stronger students to link more than two boxes together, give the weaker students vocabulary which they can use to help them link the boxes together, or leave one box in the learning grid blank to give students the freedom to choose an aspect or feature of the topic to link with the feature of another box already thrown.

> **Bonus idea** ★
>
> Instead of a learning grid that focuses on a single revision topic, fill in the boxes with short revision tasks and give students a topic to revise for 10 minutes in class. Once the 10 minutes is up, students throw the die once and then have to carry out the task in the corresponding numbered square.

#Learninggrid

Let's go shopping!

Don't spend too much!

This active teaching technique, ideal for kinaesthetic students, was inspired by Mark Cowan. It will turn your classroom into a bustling revision hypermarket.

This activity should take a whole lesson. It has the following stages.

1. Pre-prepare a list of key terms/factors associated with an issue. For history, this could be factors related to the rise of Hitler.
2. Add a price tag to each factor depending upon its importance to the topic or exam question that you are focusing on. For instance, on the topic of the Rise of Hitler you could price the Treaty of Versailles at £2, the Great Depression at £3, Proportional Representation at £1 and Hitler at £4.
3. Give the students a budget - they must decide what factors they would buy with the exam question in mind.
4. Provide a shopping list sheet for students to write down their choices and the reasons why they have chosen each factor.
5. The evaluation and class discussion for this task is crucial. Key questions to ask are 'Were the prices fair?', 'Would you adjust the prices for any factors?', 'Would you use any special offers, such as 'buy-one-get-one-free' for factors that influenced or resulted in another, and what difference would this have made to your decisions?'

It is important to suggest that completing the shopping list properly is in effect constructing an effective essay plan, with the shopping item as the theme of each paragraph and the reasons why you have selected it as the evidence and judgement to support it.

#Revisionshopping

Odd one out or odd one in?

Are you in or are you out?

This great revision activity can be used to warm up brains or check progress and provoke discussion, using skills in handling evidence and explanation.

Students should be given four or five items, as images or words on a board or sheet, which are linked to a topic. These items can be applied in a number of ways within the framework.

- Students have to devise an explanation for each item, stating how it could be seen as the odd one out.
- Students have to devise an explanation for the odd two out. This may need a longer list than five items.
- Play 'how much odd one out', where each item is compared and contrasted and students have to decide which item is the oddest one out.
- Working in groups, each group is given a separate item within the list and has to come up with as many differences as possible.
- Reverse all this and play 'odd one in', where students need to identify the similarities between the items on the list.

To reinforce the learning further, ask students to make a record what they have learned from the activity. They can do this quickly and efficiently using a graphic organiser, such as a Venn diagram or comparison alley, making a great revision aid for their notes.

All the games in the odd one out framework allow students to apply their knowledge rather than passively learn it. The ability to compare and contrast different items within a topic, and the development of explanation and reasoning skills, are essential in a revision programme.

Teaching tip

If you are using images, use a graphic photo presentation pack, such as the Moldiv app. It gives the resource you use a professional look and you can save them for future use.

Taking it further

Once students are used to this activity – it won't take long – ask them to come up with their own odd one out or odd one in quiz to use in lessons to test the class, revision partner or revision triad.

#Odd

Mark schemes

Mark schemes – the ladder of success!

It is important that students are aware of what a mark scheme is and how their work is assessed.

Teaching tip

Constantly use the key words from your mark scheme in the feedback you give students. Modelling and applying the language of the mark schemes immerses students in the language of assessment as well as sharpening the quality of your feedback, tying it closely to the demands of the examination.

As a starting point, mark schemes can show what they need to do to be successful and get to where they want to go. Constantly referring to the mark schemes is essential practice and should provide a point of reference during a revision programme. Here are a number of ways you can use mark schemes within your revision programme to enable students to fully understand them.

Break them! Cutting up mark schemes and asking students to reorder them again is a simple way of allowing students to consider the structure of a mark scheme. It also encourages them to look more closely at the progression of skills between the different levels of response. This can spark a class discussion on the skills required in the exam, as well as the differences between the responses.

Rewrite them! This activity is more suited to an exam class who are already very familiar with the mark schemes. Give the students the level headings and ask them to write a description for each level. Ask the key questions: 'What skills are required?', 'What should a Level X answer look like?', 'What is the difference between Level X and Level Y?' This is a great way of checking student understanding of exam requirements, as well as prompting a class discussion on the mark schemes without you having to dominate and lecture to your students.

#Revmarkschemes

Display them! Having the mark schemes displayed on your walls makes for an excellent revision aid and is something to refer to when giving feedback and going through model answers. Even better is to have copies of student-friendly mark schemes in students' exercise books. These make a great reference point when giving feedback and are also a handy resource for peer-assessment revision activities. To make them more attractive, rewrite them in student-friendly language and use a comic book app, such as Halftone 2, to make a striking and attention-grabbing document.

Use them! When students' work is returned, ask them to look at their copies of the mark scheme and highlight their work in different colours where they have reached the different levels of the mark scheme. This is a great, and easy to set up DIRT activity that requires students to read, use and apply the feedback you have given them with the mark scheme.

Apply them! Give students statements that would appear in an answer to an exam question. These statements could be a couple of sentences or a whole paragraph. Ask students where each statement would fit on the mark scheme. This allows students to consider the quality of the statement, assessing the language and the application of knowledge within it, as well as encouraging them to closely scrutinise of the mechanisms of a quality answer.

Bonus idea ★

Therefore, one of the first things to do with any exam class is to give them the mark schemes against which their work is judged.

Mini sagas

Once upon a time . . .

The memory has an amazing capacity to remember stories. Why not get your students to create their own revision stories in the form of mini sagas?

Mini sagas are stories that are exactly 50 words and have the same construction as a regular story: a beginning, a middle and an end. They were first promoted by Brian Aldiss and *The Telegraph* in the early 1980s. As Neil Watkin and Johannes Ahrenfelt state, mini sagas are most successful for revision purposes when they are cryptic and students must work out their meaning.

Mini sagas offer many different opportunities to explore content and provide an excellent and stimulating memory aid. They can be used in revision sessions as a starter, in order to introduce a story, a person or an event. In this context, mini sagas create curiosity and engagement at the beginning of the lesson.

However, mini sagas are most effective when students write them themselves. It is important to model a mini saga of your own first so that students know how they work. This is one I use with my Year 11 groups in revision lessons. It is about Ho Chi Minh, leader of North Vietnam.

The hope for freedom never dies

There was once a man who wanted to be free. Dreamt of beating bigger people for unity and independence. He led a secret army. Fought in clever ways, with tunnels and guns, against deadly, murderous weapons. Showed the path towards freedom for others. He died but freedom was achieved. Forever.

Once you have presented the mini saga, the class discussion should centre on these questions:

- Who is involved?
- What is the subject of the mini saga and how does this relate to the exam?
- What has been left out?
- What else could have been included?

Once students are familiar with mini sagas and their construction, they can write their own, based on any event, person or development that relates to the topic. Then, each student reads theirs out to the rest of the class, who then have to answer the questions above. Therefore, all students are involved and are simultaneously peer assessing each other's work.

For revision, mini sagas work on a number of levels:

- If students are writing their own then the OFSTED literacy box is ticked, especially as you are using creative writing as a device.
- Mini sagas can offer reviewing and revision opportunities which are different and engaging and allow for creativity.
- Mini sagas can use important source skills. In writing and evaluating mini sagas students are deploying skills, such as applying their own knowledge, to understand the meaning.

Mini sagas can work for any subject and on any topic. For example:

- Maths – the thinking process of a puzzle.
- Geography – the description of key features of volcanoes.
- Science – the stages of an experiment.
- English – the plotline of a novel.
- French and German – a story that involves key topic vocabulary.
- Religious education – the key beliefs of a world religion.

Taking it further

Collect all the mini sagas that student write, type them up and display them in the classroom. This is an unusual display which can provide a brilliant memory aid and provoke curiosity – as all stories with a mystery do.

#Minisaga

Poundland pedagogy

Revision is cheap as chips!

Poundland pedagogy shows us that high-quality revision aids and materials can be bought at bargain prices with a little bit of creativity and ingenuity.

'Poundland pedagogy' was created by Isabella Wallace and became a Twitter phenomenon before appearing in print for the first time in 2014. The idea is that cheap poundstore items can be turned into imaginative learning resources.

Here are some of the best ideas that teachers have shared on Twitter.

- Wooden craft cubes can be transformed into dice for revision board games.
- Washing lines can be used to create visual timelines, continuums or bunting to celebrate great revision.
- Plasticine can be used to make models of key learning points.
- Connector post-it notes in the shape of arrows, squares, circles and jigsaw pieces can be used to illustrate different sections of writing an essay or to create flow charts or mark schemes with responses.
- Paper plates can be used for Venn diagrams, or you can turn them into model clocks to demonstrate time management skills and how to plan time during revision schedules.
- Use egg timers for revision quizzes.
- Rolls of paper (particularly lining paper) are great for creating 'revision walls' where students can record information and create large-scale visual revision aids.
- Pegs can be used to categorise common items for a topic or to put things in order, such as a sequence of sentences.

#Poundlandpedagogy

Target practice

Well done! You are bang on target!

This activity helps students organise information visually and can summarise a revision session.

All you need is a sheet for each student with three circles in the form of a target, with a topic in the middle, like this:

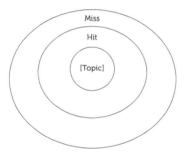

Miss
Hit
[Topic]

Give students a series of words or statements in random order – about ten is a good number. The words and statements relate to the topic written in the centre of the target. A geography example can be seen below:

Topic: Countries in Europe

Britain, United States, Brazil, Germany, Australia, Andorra, France, Burkina Faso, Spain

Students write the correct answers, in this instance the countries that are in Europe, in the 'hit' circle and the incorrect answers, in this instance the countries that are not in Europe, in the 'miss' circle. Students can swap targets and mark each other's – neatly fitting in some peer assessment.

#Targetpractice

Using model answers

Looking good!

Leading creative activities using model answers will improve student outcomes at whatever level they are working at.

Teaching tip

Don't restrict yourself to perfect model answers. Giving a student a weaker answer can highlight what mistakes can be made and what they look like in an answer. This is just as valuable as knowing what to do to reach the higher grades.

Prompting students to interact with model answers, rather than slavishly reading them and, worse still, copying them, will deepen understanding and boost chances for exam success. Here are three strategies to use model answers in an interactive, practical way.

Mark it! Using the mark scheme, students mark the model answer and then measure their mark (with explanation) against that given by the examiner. This can work for any answer, written or practical, at any level. This type of exercise sharpens student knowledge of exam criteria.

Broken answers Cut up a model answer and photocopy the 'broken' pieces onto one sheet of paper. Each student should be given a copy of the 'broken answer'; their job is to cut it up and rearrange it into its original shape. The activity helps students consider the structure of an answer more closely, and how parts of the answer fit together. For greater challenge, add annotations to the broken pieces, commenting on particular parts of the answer. Students should fit each one beside the appropriate part of the answer.

Taking it further

On the basis of using model answers, ask students to create their own based on these activities and display them in your classroom, complete with feedback indicating why they are good. This not only provides an excellent revision aid and practises essential exam skills but also boosts student motivation and gives a clear demonstration of progress.

Fill it in! Give students copies of model answers but with missing pieces for them to fill in. Try erasing the beginnings of sentences so that students can examine how to start a sentence off in different contexts, or erase key words and subject-specific vocabulary, demonstrating how particular words are used for exam answers.

#Revisionmodel

WAGOLLs

Modelling isn't the best way to teach – it is the only way to teach.

WAGOLL (What a Good One Looks Like) refers to modelling the outcome which you want your students to achieve. As Andy Griffith and Mark Burns advocate, teaching backwards is the way forward.

Using a WAGOLL is a crucial part of your revision programme. Modelling what you want your students to achieve gives them explicit and precise objectives on what they need to do to reach the highest levels in any assessment. Think of a jigsaw puzzle – it is much easier to complete it when you know what the overall image looks like. WAGOLLs can be used in a variety of contexts within a revision session and can elicit superb discussions. Here are a few examples:

- Display a WAGOLL in your classroom alongside the mark scheme and label it to show where the answer hits the different levels. You can use the myriad mock answers in revision guides with commentary for inspiration.
- Give students a WAGOLL and use Jim Smith's Biggest, Best, Beautiful structure to get students to draw out the main points. Students would need to answer what is the biggest point you could take away from the WAGOLL, what is the best point and, finally, what is the most beautiful feature of it.
- A great idea, advocated by Andy Griffith and Mark Burns, is to have a two-circle Venn diagram and place a WAGOLL in one circle. In the opposite circle, students attempt the task (such as an exam question). Where the circles overlap, students can write similarities between their own model and the WAGOLL. Outside the circle, they can list the points they need to develop.

Teaching tip

WAGOLLs are a great resource to draw on during revision time, and many are readily available from revision books and exam boards. Using them with a mark scheme focuses students on the requirements of the higher levels, regardless of the ability level. Using WAGOLLs for all students is a great way of evidencing high expectations and ambition for all students – even for those who may never reach the higher levels in your subject.

#WAGOLL

Six degrees of separation

The chain of learning!

This revision game links anything and everything and is ideal for those tricky synoptic papers students encounter at A Level.

Teaching tip

Placing a time limit can add pressure and give a competitive edge to the activity. It can also prevent the activity taking over the whole of the lesson!

Six degrees of separation – the theory that everyone and anyone is no more than six steps (or fewer) away from each other – can be used as a framework for a revision game that encourages students to link and sequence their learning, using a broad knowledge which they will need for their examinations.

The basic framework of the activity works like this:

Taking it further

This activity can be easily differentiated by increasing or decreasing the number of terms students are given to make their connection from. You could give more able students no terms to work with, so they must make their chain independently. Varying the steps within the connection chain is another way of differentiating.

Another way to differentiate is by placing a term in the middle of the chain of connection so that students have to include three (or even four for longer connections) terms within their chain.

- Split your class into teams or pairs, depending on how you want to conduct the activity. This can also be done as a whole class activity as an extended plenary exercise.
- Give the students between 10 and 14 terms or words from a topic - these can be written on the board, or given to students in packs of cards with the terms or words on them.
- On the board, clearly write two more terms or words related to the topic. In groups or pairs, ask the students to make a chain of connection between the terms or words you have given them and the two written on the board. Students have to make six steps in their chain of connection. However, this can be altered depending on how difficult you want to make the activity.
- To add competition, explain that the first team or pair to complete the task can only win if they are able to correctly explain the links between each of the six connections. This stage is extremely important as it enables you to check students can fully understand and explain their ideas. It also adds an element of peer assessment, as the other students have to assess the quality of the links made.

#6degsep

Revision and the memory

Part 4

Active revision

See it, hear it, touch it, feel it, read it, smell it, say it, DO IT!

Revision must be an active process. Using a theoretical base to support decisions on revision activities is crucial in planning a balanced and effective revision programme that helps your students perform at their very best.

To encourage greater awareness of this theory, always ask students where different revision activities fit within this memory framework. This will increase their awareness and understanding on the theory, and help them consider the effectiveness of certain revision strategies. Implementing this framework while planning revision sessions ensures maximum impact, both for students and teachers.

Training the memory and enabling your students to recall and apply information is vital in a robust revision programme. Making revision 'stick' must be the overall objective and creating memory triggers is an important way of achieving it. Many theorists argue that creating memory triggers requires a multi-sensory experience. From this work, a framework has been put together which looks at the percentages of information retained in correlation to how the information is processed. This framework is often shown as a pyramid, or as a cone of learning, like this:

Practise by reading
Memory retains 10% after two weeks

Practise by hearing
Memory retains 20% after two weeks

Demonstration
Memory retains 30% after two weeks

Practise by seeing and hearing
Memory retains 50% after two weeks

Practise by saying
Memory retains 70% after two weeks

Teaching others/immediate use of learning
Memory retains 90% after two weeks

This is a very handy framework to work around when you are planning activities for a revision programme, as it helps you focus on the revision process rather than the revision products and outcomes. It also helps you to move away from some of the more traditional revision approaches, such as lectures and notemaking, and take a more interactive approach, which helps students retain information more effectively.

To encourage independence, share this pyramid with students and parents. Tell them that this is the theoretical background with which you are working to improve their knowledge. Regularly revisit this when you are completing revision activities and ask students where the activity fits on the pyramid. Continually reminding students about this framework shows them not only that you treat them like adults but also why you have chosen revision activities. Exposing students to this reasoning allows them to make better choices of activities when they are revising independently.

Taking it further

Have this pyramid on regular display and refer to it. One way to introduce it is to give students a copy of the pyramid and ask them to write on each layer of the pyramid the activities that fit the description of that layer. Share this as a class and as a result you will have a whole list of memory effective activities that they can incorporate into their revision programme. Also, it illustrates that simply reading content, without doing something with it, is not an effective way of revising.

#Activerev

Bodily revision

Now where does this fit?

All memory stems from the power of association. This memory technology uses parts of the body to help revise key information.

Visualisation is an effective way to sharpen the memory. Using the body as a memory training technique can give your students a fun and powerful revision method.

Give your students ten items of knowledge linked to a specific topic – present them on the whiteboard. Give them a minute to try to lock them in their memory. Once the minute is over, hide the ten items and then ask them how many they can remember.

Next, ask the students to visualise someone they know very well. Ask your students to place each of the items from the first stage on a particular part of the body they are visualising, starting with the head and working downwards. For example, if the students were revising the Cold War, it could look like this:

- Imagine Truman Doctrine on the top of your head.
- Imagine Containment in the mouth.
- Imagine 1962 nuclear weapons along the arms.
- Imagine the Berlin Wall around the throat.
- Imagine the Iron Curtain across the chest.
- Imagine Cuba tattooed on the stomach.
- Imagine Castro popping out of your belly button.
- Imagine Reagan on your right leg.
- Imagine Gorbachev on your left leg.

Finally, ask the students how many of the items they can remember now. Compare this with the number remembered in the initial stage of the activity.

Brain breaks

Make sure you don't break your brain by using a brain break . . .

Brain breaks, advocated by the University of the First Age, encourage stimulation of the brain through changing the physical and mental state of students so that they stay alert and focused.

Revision sessions can be intense. Ensuring the brain is stimulated and focused is key to making a session effective. Brain breaks are short exercises that use movement and help students concentrate for longer. Here are a few to try.

Thumb up, finger out!

- Ask students to hold both hands in front of them in fists.
- With one hand, raise the thumb and with the other extend the little finger out to the side.
- Now swap over, so that the hand with the thumb raised now extends the finger and vice versa.

One, two, three

- Students work in pairs and stand opposite each other. They need to count to three, each saying a number in turn. Allow a minute or two for them to do this continuously.
- Replace 'one' with a clap; two' with a stamp and 'three' with a 'grr. Allow students to practise.

Alive, awake, alert!

- Everyone stands up, preferably in a circle.
- Introduce the words and the actions.
- Chant: Alive, alert, awake! Enthusiastic!
- Actions: Alive = both hands on head.
  Alert = hands on both shoulders.
  Awake = arms crossing chest.
  Enthusiastic = tap legs, clap hands and click fingers.

> **Bonus idea** ★
>
> **Flat hand, pointy finger**
> In pairs, students face each other, raise their right hands and point a finger. The open left palm is held upwards. The pointed finger should be held above the open palm of the other person without touching it. When the teacher says 'Go!', the object of the activity is to grab the pointed finger of your partner, while avoiding your pointed finger being grabbed by them.

#Brainbreak

Colour my revision

Revision does not necessarily have to be black or white.

This engaging technique brings a little colour to your revision sessions and encourages students to think laterally.

Taking it further

Once students have got used to this activity and know how it works, allow them to choose their own colours to apply their knowledge to and, once they have completed an agreed number, let them circulate and swap answers. This is great collaborative learning with minimal effort on your part.

All you need for this technique is a list of colours. Anything between five and ten will do, depending on how long you want to spend on the activity. It makes a splendid plenary at the end of a session, where you can test student knowledge as well as allowing them to apply this in a fun and interesting way.

Start by giving the students a list of colours, either on sheets of paper or on the board. Students need to work through the list of colours and explain why each one is relevant to the topic. For example, this is a list of colours applied to the topic of the Treaty of Versailles.

Red represents Germans' at being forced to sign the Treaty and therefore being blamed for the causing the First World War.

White represents the fact that the Treaty of Versailles was the peace agreement between the Allies and Germany.

Black represents the mood of the Germans who felt that they had been 'stabbed in the back' by their new leaders.

Blue represents the nationalistic attitude of the French who wanted to punish Germany.

Knowledge is clearly applied within the task rather than copied out. It can also relieve a little bit of stress and introduce some fun into an intense revision session, while retaining a focus and developing important revision skills.

#Revisioncolour

Context dependent learning

Say what you see . . .

Making links and connections is the basis of all memory training. Context dependent learning gets students in the mood for revision and is also perfect exam preparation for the 'real thing'.

Central to high-quality memory training is the power of association. For revision purposes, this means getting students to remember information by linking it with what they encounter every day, such as colours and music. Sir Timothy Brighouse suggests bringing this form of memory training sharply into a revision programme with what he calls context dependent learning.

Brighouse advocates this by taking your exam classes to the location where they may take their exam, be that the main school hall or gym, and use it as the location of a revision session. You should make use of the surrounding environment and make links with the content that needs to be revised. For example, information on the Iron Curtain could be linked with the curtains on the stage, or the colours of the room linked with scientific experiments.

Modelling this way of memory training gives your students working examples that they can use in the actual exam location, as well as other locations where they are revising. Context dependent learning is very similar to the locus methods of learning (locus is Latin for 'place' or 'location') and brings this ancient way of recalling material into a modern context. Another impact of this method is that it accustoms students to the exam location so that they are fully prepared for the day of the examination.

Taking it further

Context dependent learning can cater for all different learning styles. Encourage your students to rehearse the information they associate with the exam location verbally, either as a list or a journey around the room, get them to walk around the exam location making physical connections with the information and features of the room, to make a visual journey through the location, associating information with different items.

Bonus idea ★

Choose a random everyday object, such as a vase or a tin opener, and ask students to link that object to the information they need to revise. You will be guaranteed some interesting answers, and the students will be applying and discussing the information that they are revising, therefore training that all-important memory.

#Cdl

Making your revision RING

Ding dong!

Going over old material can provoke the 'we've done this before!' reaction. Keeping Dave Keeling's RING principle in mind when planning revision activities can be very useful in making such lessons engaging and active at all times.

RING stands for **R**elevant, **I**nteresting, **N**aughty, **G**iggle. To apply this in revision lessons:

Make your revision **relevant:** make it clear that the content you are covering may appear in the exam, and that the skills you are developing are highly important. This addresses the crucial element of 'what is in it for me?'

Make your revision **interesting**: present revision materials in an attention-grabbing way, promoting engagement to ensure that students are interested and want to learn. You'll find lots of activities in this book to help you do this.

Make your revision **naughty**: be daring and try something new! Who wants a revision session that contains the same tired old activities? If a new activity doesn't work, try something else. If it does, you are on to a winner!

Make your revision a **giggle**: if students are engaged and enjoying themselves then they are willing to learn more, and the more their confidence soars, and that is worth aiming for. Many of the activities in this book promote engagement and enjoyment as well as effective revision.

As Dave Keeling says, having one of these elements will probably mean that students will remember most of what you have taught them, but to have all four means that they will never forget it – and that is what revision is all about.

#RING

Map from memory

Mapping your knowledge is essential for finding your way to great revision!

This activity encourages students to revise collaboratively and makes the most out of visual resources to sharpen the memory.

This is very easy to prepare and allows students to take centre stage. You will need a visual resource – this can be a pre-prepared mind map, a diagram relevant to the subject being revised, such as a skeleton, a timeline or the periodic table.

Divide your students into groups of three, and give each student a number - one, two or three. Call up all the number ones. These students have 30 seconds to study the visual resource, memorising as much as they can. Place the diagrams somewhere that no other students can see. Once the 30 seconds is up, the students return back to their groups and explain what they have seen to the rest of the group, who start to create a picture based on the information on the team's large piece of paper. Repeat this process with the second and third members of the team. The aim is for students to recreate the visual resource as accurately as possible.

This activity helps train the memory as well as encouraging students to explain to each other what information they have seen, plugging the gaps of each other's knowledge and reduce their dependence on the teacher, who for this activity, acts as a facilitator.

It is essential that all the groups' diagrams are shared and the class can decide which one was the most accurate. Sharing the diagrams provides great stimulus for discussion and can help fill any remaining gaps in their knowledge.

Taking it further

Extend this by appointing students to choose the diagram for the activity from a range of choices. They can then explain to the rest of the class why they have chosen it to revise from. Deploy these same students during the activity as your 'policemen', and check that there is no cheating going on – this is especially useful if you place the diagrams out in the corridor.

#Memorymap

Revision and music

If the food of revision is music, play on!

Recent research has shown that using music in the right way can improve memory and recall, and aid learning. Therefore, effectively using music in your revision programme will help your students learn and also increase engagement and motivation.

Nina Jackson's work on using music in the classroom has become increasingly influential over the last few years. Her work is practical and helpful, and well worth adding to your revision toolbox.

Given extensive exposure to the right music while studying, students will be able to develop associations between the selected music and specific information. This also helps with using all the senses to revise and take information in, making memory and recall far more effective.

In achieving this, Nina Jackson has identified clear steps to ensure that music can enhance effective revision and learning:

- Explain clearly what you want your students to revise and while they go through the information, play your chosen music.
- Stop the music when you think your students have had enough time. Then ask the students to present what they think are the key points from the information in a way which is easy for them to remember.
- Then ask them to revise the same material again with the same extract of music. Because they have made links with the music and content, they are far more likely to remember the content.
- To reinforce this further, play the music again at the end of the revision session at a low volume and ask your students to present their key learning points to another student.

#Musicrev

Pomodoro technique

Prevent your revision being blocked by rotten tomatoes!

The Pomodoro technique, created by Francesco Cirillo, is a great tool for improving productivity, time management and organising tasks.

The Pomodoro technique is increasingly being used as a framework to help students organise their work and manage their time effectively. The technique helps students to establish what their most important work is and to work in short, sharp sessions with frequent breaks to maximise attention spans. The Pomodoro in this instance is a tomato shaped kitchen timer, which Cirillo used to develop the technique, and it is the name he uses to identify a unit of time spent on a specific task.

Firstly, decide what topics are going to be revised and what tasks need to be completed which then need to be ordered in importance in a to-do list, for example:

- recite French vocabulary topic on travel – 20 mins;
- complete ten questions on fractions – 20 mins;
- complete write up on biology experiment – 20 mins;
- practise piece for music assessment – 20 mins.

When your students have created a plan, they should time themselves for each task. The amount of time devoted to each task depends on how long students can concentrate for. When they hear the alarm, students stop the task, take a short break of up to five minutes, and tick off the completed Pomodoro on the table. If students complete the task early, they can go through it again. After four rounds, students should take a longer break of up to half an hour, before starting again.

Teaching tip

To get students used to this framework of managing time and concentration, model it in a revision session, where you set four short and sharp tasks which they have to complete according to the Pomodoro model.

#Pomodoro

Sharpening the memory

Make your learning stick!

Developing and finding ways to improve the memory is central to a successful revision programme and exam performance.

#Revsharp

The University of the First Age produces many fantastic resources that promote and help develop an effective memory, such as:

- **Create an interest** Make clear the benefits and relevance of the information to students' exam performance. This means their memory will be more attuned to absorbing relevant information.
- **Create associations** Use techniques that link new and previous learning. Helping the brain to recall what it already knows increases the chances of remembering new information.
- **Rehearse out loud** Encourage your students to speak and perform.
- **Build in unusual information** The brain remembers anything different, strange or funny. Build this into your programme, for example by using revision games.
- **Return to the learning regularly** Reviewing information aids memory. Use strategies such as post-it notes, flash cards and mind maps.
- **Organise information into chunks** Encourage students to learn information in 'chunks', rather than in overwhelming sections. The chunking triangle can help with this.
- **Concentrate** The brain can only absorb information in short bursts. Encourage students to work for 16 to 20 minutes, then stand up, stretch, and walk around. Try the Brain Gym or the Pomodoro technique.
- **Use pictures** Encourage students to draw and use colour. The brain takes in images and colour much better than words.

AMGIAM – Acronyms and Mnemonics Great In Aiding Memory

TSMW – Thanks Sir! More Work!

Acronyms and mnemonics are brilliant tools for brain training and memory skills. They should be in every teacher's toolkit.

Acronyms, mnemonics and acrostics are fabulous ways of training the memory. The brain disregards 70% of what you learn in a day within 24 hours, so students must develop techniques to remember key information.

Mnemonics refer to a sentence in which the initial letters of each word provide an aid to remembering something in a particular order. For example, 'My Very Educated Mother Just Served Us Nine Pizzas' can help us remember the planets in the Milky Way in order, while 'Rhythm Helps Your Two Hips Move' can help you remember the spelling of rhythm.

An acronym is an abbreviation formed from the initial components in a phrase or a word. These components may be individual letters (as in DIY) or parts of words (as in Benelux). For some courses, students have to learn them as part of the content, such as NATO – North Atlantic Treaty Organisation – so why not utilise these skills as part of students' revision toolkit?

Students should be encouraged to make up their own mnemonics and acronyms. It is far easier to remember these than a whole tract of text and is an immensely valuable revision skill. Not only that, but students will already know what the mnemonic or acronym means before they use it because they cut the content down.

Taking it further

An effective task is to give students an acronym based on the content of the lesson, then ask them to decipher what the acronym means based on the key learning points of the lesson. For example, when teaching a lesson on the Treaty of Versailles, give students the acronym LAMB at the beginning of the lesson. By the middle or end of the lesson they will need to find out what LAMB means. For the record, LAMB means Land, Army, Money, Blame.

#AMGIAM

Active revision

Part 5

Reconstruction DARTs

Making sure revision hits double top!

DARTs (Directed Activities Related to Texts) are a collection of activities that help students engage with texts on a deeper level. These are vital in any revision programme that requires students to process significant amounts of information from text-based material.

DARTs were developed in the 1970s and 1980s by Eric Lunzer and Keith Gardner, and became extremely popular in classrooms. Reconstruction DARTs activities require students to engage with text by filling in missing sections or sequencing material that has been mixed up. Here are a few ideas.

Missing subheadings Give your students photocopies from a textbook with the subheadings erased and ask students what these should be. Then, compare them with the actual subheadings. The student-created subheadings also become a ready-made summary of the topic.

Jumbled up answers Cut up a model exam answer and ask the students to reconstruct it. This encourages them to look at the language used and to consider how paragraphs connect. Some revision guides with model exam answers also contain examiner annotations. Cut these up, and ask students to place them beside the relevant section of the answer.

Key word gap fill Give students a summary of a topic with the key words missing. Students need to fill in the gaps. This reinforces the subject-specific vocabulary students need to use in examinations.

Table completion Give students a half-completed table of information that summarises a topic. With the given text, students complete the table. Or, give students a completed table with the headings missing and ask them to complete them.

Analysis DARTs

Making sure your revision hits the bullseye!

Analysis DARTs get students thinking more analytically.

Analysis DARTs activities encourage students to locate and categorise relevant information by labelling or marking a text or a diagram. Students have to sort information, consider its relevance to a set objective and evaluate what they are reading – all essential skills. Below is a selection of analysis DARTs exercises.

Answering comprehension questions Give students a text with accompanying questions to answer using the source. These questions can be sourced and framed in different ways:

- teacher sets the questions based on knowledge gathering that require short answers.
- students set questions based on the text for each other in pairs or groups.
- teacher sets open-ended questions which require analysis and higher-order thinking.

Text marking Give students a text in which they have to underline information with a specific meaning. For example, ask them to underline the five words that summarise the topic, or subject-specific vocabulary or connective words, that improve the quality of the writing.

Diagram and cartoons Students design a diagram or cartoon that represents the meaning of a text.

Summarising text Students have to summarise a text in a given word limit.

Converting text Students have to convert a text into a different format. For example, into a flow chart.

Teaching tip

These activities require little preparation apart from deciding upon the text and choosing the activity. It would be a good idea to give students an example of the outcome you want them to achieve so they have a clear idea of the task objectives.

Taking it further

Once your students have practised a range of analysis DARTs, give them a text and allow them to choose which analysis DARTs to tackle. This creates a sense of ownership of the session.

Bonus idea ★

Colourful text
Give students three questions and ask them to underline the information that answers them in three different colours. Or give them a mark scheme and a model answer, and ask them to underline where the answer hits the different levels within the mark scheme, with a colour for each level.

#ANDARTS

Hexagons

Can I have a P please teacher?

Hexagonal learning is an idea championed by David Didau – The Learning Spy – as way for students to access the SOLO (Structure of the Observed Learning Outcome) taxonomy. SOLO is a means of classifying learning outcomes in terms of their complexity. Hexagon learning provides students with a linked overview of a topic.

Give students a sheet with diagrams of 12 to 16 hexagons. Each hexagon contains a word on a given topic. For example, if you are teaching prohibition, you may include 'speakeasies', 'bootleggers' and 'gangsters'. Students need to cut out the hexagons; their natural response should be to fit the hexagons together. Every time a student aligns two hexagons they must explain the link or connection between the two words.

This activity allows for a wide range of individual responses and many different patterns to be made. The ultimate aim is to see how many sides of each hexagon you can get to touch. Hexagon learning allows students to produce a visual summary of a topic, which they can refer to when revising. It also gives them an overview of both the content and how they applied their knowledge in making and explaining links across a topic – a crucial skill for exam success.

Here are other ways to apply hexagon learning activities as part of a revision programme:

- give students some blank hexagons - how should they fill them?
- ask students to make a hexagon pattern without writing their links down. Then students swap hexagon patterns and write the links from their partner's pattern.

#Revhex

Cause, event and effect

It is all about organisation.

The cause, event and effect framework is a visual organiser that organises information under potential exam questions and areas.

The organiser is structured like this:

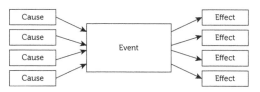

This kind of framework helps students to classify facts as causes, events or effects, essential for subjects such as history, English, economics and psychology. Information organised in this way is a ready-made checklist that students can use for the different types of questions that they may face.

Give students short bullet points on cards that sum up a topic, such as these points on the topic of the Berlin Blockade and Airlift:

- Russian planes flew up against USA planes supplying Berlin.
- USA, Britain and France introduced a united currency in their Berlin zones.
- USA decided upon launching Operation Vittle in June 1948.
- Germany divided into West Germany and East Germany in 1949.

Ask students to organise their bullet points into the cause, event and effect framework. This active revision activity makes an interesting alternative to a mind map, and produces an exam-focused visual revision aid.

Teaching tip

Always have blank cause, event and effect frameworks to hand. Use A3 size paper for pair work and sugar paper size for group work – this enables all students to contribute quickly and easily. Using large paper makes it easy for groups to present their findings to the rest of the class in the debrief.

Taking it further

In many examinations that test this type of knowledge, judgements are required about importance and significance. Build this into the activity by asking your students to order the different causes and effects by significance, adding a degree of judgement as well as recall.

#CEE

Diamond nine

Cutting edge revision . . .

Diamond nine is a popular classroom activity that promotes evaluation and explanation, helps develop essential skills tested in exams and should have a place in all revision toolkits.

This activity helps students to reach substantiated judgements about different features and items of the topic. You can use it quickly by preparing a PowerPoint slide or by writing the revision topic on the board and nine related items. If you have more time, make sets of cards with nine related items on.

For this activity students, in pairs, have to rank nine items of information related to a topic in order of importance in the shape of a diamond nine. The most important item should be positioned at the top, two items in the second row, three in the third, two in the fourth and the least important one in the fifth. Then students have to explain and justify their decisions. Ranking material is something they must do in exams. You can vary this activity to make it more interesting and challenging:

- Give students more than nine items. Which items would they leave out of their diamond nine and why?
- Working in pairs, give students a set of nine blank cards, each with a given topic or question to revise. Ask them to write related information, then swap sets and diamond nine rank each other's card sets.
- Present a completed diamond nine diagram and ask your students to write three points justifying the decisions made and three points attacking the decisions.
- Ask students if they can justify placing each item at the top of the diamond nine.

#Diamond9

Energisers

When the going gets tough, the tough get boosted . . .

Energisers are quick, short activities that are designed to lift spirits, boost energy and raise alertness.

In any revision session energy levels can plummet and students can lose interest. Throwing in a different activity to refocus students can make the challenge of continuing to revise much more realistic. Energisers are activities designed to give students a boost and relieve pressure. Here are two examples.

Bob!

- Students sit or stand silently in a circle.
- Students 'bob down' in turns. The first to bob down says 'one', the second says 'two' and so on.
- If more than one person bobs down then everyone has to stand up and start again.
- The game ends when everyone is down.

Sentence relay

- Divide the class into teams of six. The teams will compete to be the first to complete a sentence. They have to write the sentence on the board or a piece of paper pinned up at the opposite end of the room. Each group is assigned a sentence on a revision topic.
- In turn, each team member adds one word to the sentence. No words can be inserted between words already in the sentence.
- Each team has one marker. Markers take turns to run to the board, write their word, then pass the marker to the next person.
- Give teams a debriefing at the end to review each team's sentence.

> **Teaching tip**
>
> When using energisers, always explain why you are using them and what you are trying to achieve. Otherwise, students can easily see them as a game without any real learning purpose.

#Energiser

Mind maps

I know where I am going now, Miss!

Mind maps, created by Tony Buzan, stimulate both right and left hemispheres of the brain. A mind map's use of colour, language, logic and images make it an excellent aid for the memory.

Teaching tip

When you first use mind maps with a class, get the students to design one about themselves. Then ask students to exchange their mind maps with a fellow student, who marks it in accordance to the key features list. This encourages peer assessment as well as marking to an agreed list like an exam mark scheme.

Taking it further

There are some great online tools to make attractive and accessible mind maps. Amongst the most effective are Simple Mind, which can be used on desktops, tablets and phones, and Popplet, which is a great app for the tablet.

Bonus idea ★

Ask students, to create their own mind maps on different sections of a given exam topic and then ask them to present their mind maps to the class.

#Mindmaps4rev

The key features of a mind map are:

- A central image forms the subject of the mind map.
- Main themes radiate from the middle represented by branches. Branches are curved and the thickness of a branch should reflect the importance of its theme.
- Only key words and images are used; which stimulates the brain.
- Lots of space is required and it should all fit onto one side of paper – either A4 or A3 size.

Mind maps enable students to link content, are time-effective, incorporate different learning styles and are a great way to review lots of content.

To make them even more interactive you could use mind maps in the following ways:

- Leave the image out and ask students to work out the theme.
- Can students justify the importance of each key word? Are there other key words that should be included and others left out?
- For the less able, create a basic mind map framework and them a list of key words that they need to fit onto it.
- For the more able, create a basic mind map on an exam topic and ask your students to draw as many links as possible and explain their choice of links.

Prepare like an American president

What is urgent is seldom important and what is important is seldom urgent.

This is a prioritising tool straight from the White House, and it may help your students organise revision tasks effectively.

Being able to prioritise revision tasks is an important step in becoming a successful learner. The Eisenhower Matrix, named after the American president is one tool that can help you train your students to meet this target. It is presented as a square divided into quadrants, with tasks being listed in each quadrant related to their urgency and importance. The quadrants are:

Not urgent and important Tasks relating to revision goals that are not urgently necessary. These often relate to tasks that need to be completed little and often, to gradually chip away at a larger revision goal.

Urgent and important Tasks that need to be completed quickly. These are often short-term tasks that refer to last-minute preparation for the exams, such as students ensuring that they have the right equipment.

Not urgent and not important Things that may be distractions from successful revision, such as watching TV, to help students identify potential barriers to effective revision.

Urgent and not important Actions that may lead to interruptions. Ask students to identify potential interruptions, then ask what they should do when faced with these.

Teaching tip

Exploring this method of prioritising makes for a great study skills lesson and provokes interesting discussion on what is urgent and what is important when preparing for exams and assessments.

Taking it further

One way of allowing your students to familiarise themselves with this method of prioritising is to present the Eisenhower Matrix and then give your students a list of revision tasks and actions which they have to fit on their own copy of an Eisenhower Matrix. This can be done individually, in pairs or in groups; they can then present their matrices to each other, justifying their decisions.

#Preplikepres

3-minute revision motivators

That was fun!

3-minute motivators are ideal for reviewing learning and can be dropped into any revision session for any subject.

Taking it further

Once students have got used to these activities, ask them to choose one for the end of the lesson and lead it for the class.

The term 3-Minute Motivator was created by Kathy Paterson in her book of the same name. 3-minute motivators are short activities designed to break up learning. One of the main aims is for students to review their own learning, which is ideal for mixing up a revision session. Here are some examples.

Graffiti wall A graffiti wall can be used throughout revision as a place to show how well the session is going. Flip-chart paper can be put on the wall, with a heading or question on each, e.g. 'Attention level', 'Do I really understand it?', 'How this links with other topics!' This can help you monitor student understanding, address any misconceptions and fill any gaps in knowledge.

Double wheel The class forms two circles of equal numbers, one inside the other. The circles must rotate in opposite directions until the teacher says 'stop'. Then, students ask the person opposite them questions about the topic.

Runaround This quiz is based on the old children's TV show *Runaround*. Place TRUE and FALSE signs opposite each other in the room or hall. When you read a statement out, students have to move to either the true or false sign, based on what they think about the statement you have just read. Any students who go for the wrong option are out of the game, while those who are correct remain in. Repeat until you have one student left in the game.

#3minmotivator

Quick sentence For this activity ask a student to come up with a number between say, 5 and 10, then ask each student to write a sentence about the topic that has been revised with the chosen number of words. You could use a die to add a touch of randomness, especially if you use an unusual die with 10 or 12 sides.

Headings Students are given revision notes with no headings or subheadings, but with space for them to be inserted. Students must read the notes and decide on appropriate headings that summarise what follows in that section of text (headings can be in the form of a statement or a question). This produces headings such as 'Key principles of unique selling points' or 'Vocabulary for shopping in a French market'. To limit preparation time, without compromising learning outcomes, you can easily adapt existing revision notes by removing headings and asking the students to guess what the actual headings were.

Call my bluff In pairs or threes, students are given a key word or item of knowledge and have to come up with the correct meaning and two false meanings. The other groups have to spot the right answer.

Spot the mistake Present a summary of a topic that is being revised with a number of deliberate mistakes. The students have to spot the mistakes and indicate what the actual answers are.

Question before last Straight from the Mastermind sketch from The Two Ronnies, this revision activity gets students playing a game at the end of the lesson in two large teams. The teacher reads out the questions and the students must attempt to answer the question before. So the first question will not require an answer, the second question will require the answer to the first and so on.

Revision tapas

I'll have that one and this one.

Jim Smith introduced tapas learning in his book Follow Me, I'm Right Behind You. This approach can easily be adopted into your revision programme with a little thought and preparation.

Tapas learning transfers the notion of choosing what you want in whatever order you wish. Jim Smith talks about how this can be done generally in classrooms, but it can easily be used for revision.

In tapas revision sessions, you prepare a list of revision tasks that students can complete. The students choose which tasks they will tackle, which gives them a choice in how they demonstrate their learning and progress. The challenge for teachers is to list tasks encompassing a broad range of learning styles. There are a myriad of activities in this book to include in your tapas revision menu.

Allowing students to choose what and how they are going to revise immediately encourages them to think about revision and what methods suit their style of learning. Invest time beforehand in training students in a whole variety of revision methods and exercises. These will then make up your tapas revision menu and students will already be familiar with the choices on offer, allowing them to make informed decisions on what to complete and, therefore, maximising time and outcomes.

Another benefit is that students feel in control of their own learning, rather than having a set pattern of revision methods. Tapas revision encourages and promotes independence, making it more likely that effective revision will take place – both in and out of the classroom.

Bonus idea ★

Allow students to make up their own revision tapas menu for someone else. They name the topic and the activities and then create the list. You collect them, giving you a bank of revision tapas menus for students.

#Revisiontapas

Revision souvenirs

Roll up! Roll up! Get your revision souvenirs here!

Everyone loves a souvenir that reminds them of happy times. Why not transfer this memorable item for revision purposes?

Souvenirs are ubiquitous. Whether you go to a see a football match, a play or a concert, you will be given the opportunity to buy a wide range of souvenirs to remind you of the experience. If souvenirs are designed to provoke memories of such experiences, then why can't they work for learning too?

Creating a souvenir for revision is a great way of capturing learning experiences of key course content; it can be a permanent revision resource that can be referred back to long after the experience happened. This need not be just restricted to key course content, but can be extended to highlight key exam dates and related information.

Some effective revision souvenirs are:

- bookmarks with key exam information, such as dates and content of each paper.
- key rings with key topic headings summarised in an acronym.
- postcards with key content summarised in an image.
- plasticine models of important content or equipment.

These allow your students to personalise their revision materials and take control of their revision, so that they are not over-reliant on you. It is essential to create a prompt sheet with a list of ideas and suggestions. When you go through this with the students, they will fly with the ideas and will soon be creating their own revision souvenirs independently.

Teaching tip

There is no need to reinvent the wheel here. A quick search on Twitter can throw up some wonderful examples of revision souvenirs that can be either replicated or downloaded and used straight away.

Bonus idea ★

Instead of students creating their own revision souvenirs, why not encourage them to make one for somebody else. Hold a 'bring and buy exchange' where everyone in the class has to provide a revision souvenir to exchange. This gives students a perfect opportunity to collaborate in their learning as well as (surreptitiously) peer assessing each other's work while exchanging.

#Revisionsouvenir

Sell it!

Roll up! Roll Up! Get your knowledge here!

Being able to show examiners what you know is an important skill that all your students need to master to reach the highest grades.

An important part of our job when preparing students for assessments is to ensure that they can present themselves in the best possible light. These skills can be compared with sales techniques; in both cases you need to promote selected information, be persuasive and apply particular knowledge to an audience – in our case the examiners.

Design a small advert for an object Ask students to design an advert for the local newspaper selling a chosen object related to your exam course – this could range from the Berlin Wall or an equilateral triangle to a volcano or an outfit for a drama production. Place a limit on the number of words used and ask students to consider their object's unique selling point.

Design slogans and logos Give students source material that relates to what they need to revise. From this material, ask students to create realistic slogans and logos to promote the key points, topics, people or movements within the content.

Revision jingle Ask students to create a revision jingle to summarise the key points of a topic. This is great for musically talented students and you can easily increase the challenge by asking students to create a jingle for a specific type of radio show, for example, a chat show or a news programme.

Bonus idea ★

Tagline Give students an object, event, person or principle. Ask them to conjure up a tagline that would help persuade people to buy it. This is a very short, quick activity that asks students to apply their knowledge and show their learning in a limited timeframe. It is ideal as part of an end of lesson summary of key learning points.

Revision auction This activity is inspired by the wonderful television programme Bargain Hunt. Give students an object, details of an important figure, event or principle to revise. Then students, in pairs, prepare a very short presentation where they present the item as if they were selling it at an auction. Prompt students by asking what they think the asking price should be and what its unique selling points are.

#Sellit

Speed dating

Will you tick my revision?

This interactive revision activity can help get all your students talking about revision and sharing what they know.

Taking the structure of speed dating and applying it to a revision session can help you add variety to your revision programme and encourage your students to focus upon each other as a revision resource. The purpose is to revise information via straightforward peer interaction.

The process of speed dating is simple. The classroom should be arranged so that there is an equal number of chairs in parallel rows, facing each other. Split your class into two equal groups; group A sits on one row and B on the other. Group A must ask ask five questions about a specific topic; the students in group B then have to answer them. If the content of a revised topic is quite narrow, allow students in group A to choose their questions from a range of linked topics. Once you have given the signal to go (a whistle is good for this) students must talk in pairs, moving seats at regular timed intervals – if there is enough time, allow your students to make a complete circuit around the classroom and swap roles, with group B students setting the questions for group A to answer.

This activity helps students to develop important skills for their examinations, such as imparting knowledge in limited time and asking relevant and focused questions, and it also hones skills for the outside world, such as interview skills.

At the end, discuss what knowledge has been revised as well as asking students how they constructed relevant questions.

Teaching tip

To save time when carrying out this activity, ask your students to prepare five questions prior to the speed dating lesson. Don't reveal what the questions are for beforehand to add a touch of curiosity and mystery.

Taking it further

Some students may find the whole 'dating' aspect of the activity difficult and uncomfortable, so it may be wise to play down the speed dating parallel when explaining the structure of the activity.

#Revisionspeeddating

Talking revision

Chat away!

Revision should always be an active process. These two revision games help students to apply their knowledge and revise effectively.

What's inside my head A handy revision game that can also be used to review learning.

- Think of a key word, event, idea or character related to a topic you want to revise.
- Ask students to guess what you are thinking about by, firstly, writing 1, 2 and 3 on separate lines on a piece of paper.
- Give three clues to the class in three rounds, giving students the time to guess after each clue. Clue one should be very broad, with clues two and three becoming gradually more focused. Beside 1, 2 and 3 students should write down what they think you are referring to.
- Students can guess individually or in teams.

What's the question An effective revision game that encourages students to think about questions instead of answers.

- On the board, write three facts or key words linked to a topic. For example, if you were studying the key features of the Sikh faith, these could be Langar, Khanda and Khalsa.
- For each key word, students need to think of a question that the word would be an answer to. Have sentence starters on display to assist students in framing their questions.
- Share questions in a class discussion.

This game allows students to revise the content of a topic and think about how questions are framed and created — a crucial skill for understanding an exam paper.

Teach it!

Well done Mum! You got 6 out of 10. Better luck next time!

Involving parents and other adults is invaluable in an effective and practical revision programme. It shows that that we are all supporting the child to get the best possible exam results.

This task encourages collaboration between students and adults, and promotes an active approach to revision. The first stage, which can be done in lessons or at home requires the student to create a revision resource based on a selected topic. Some ideas are:

- a multiple choice quiz;
- a gap fill exercise;
- a diagram with missing labels;
- a jumbled up timeline.

Once the resource is completed, ask students to check each other's for mistakes and quality to add an element of peer assessment. When the resource has been checked, students must spend up to ten minutes teaching an adult the selected content, using notes or diagrams, reading a section of the textbook together or showing a presentation. Then the student and adult complete the resource made by the student and evaluate their performance, either based on a mark scheme provided by you or from the answers provided by the student when creating their resource. Students share their results in a debriefing class discussion in the following lesson.

This activity promotes involvement from home or from another adult, which can be a significant motivation factor for students. Letting students choose the form of the resource allows them to personalise their learning as well as including the consideration of 'how I learn' and 'what works best for me?'

Teaching tip

This activity requires a strong knowledge of your students' home backgrounds. It relies upon parents being supportive, which might not be the case for all. To avoid this potential difficulty, present the activity so that students have to teach an adult, rather than just their parents. As a safety net, ask members of your department or other adults within the school community, such as support staff, if they are willing to participate. Then direct students who are unable to find an adult to those supportive staff.

Taking it further

Add an element of competition by asking the pair to complete the task separately after the teaching session, with the challenge that the student must outperform the adult. This can add motivation as well as an extra dimension of competition within the debriefing.

#Teachit

Totem poles of revision

There is no Sitting Bull for this revision task . . .

Totem poles have been used as representations of learning by the University of the First Age, Tim Shelton and Amjad Ali, and can easily be applied as a kinaesthetic revision activity.

To add an further layer of higher-order thinking and revision, ask students to prioritise the important points of the topic by placing them in order on the totem pole, with the most important point at the top and the least important point the bottom. They should provide a one-sentence justification for each prioritised piece of information.

This activity requires a little preparation on your part, you must simply gather items that students can use to create a totem pole. To create the totem pole, tape a roll of wallpaper backing paper to the wall to make a two-metre-high pole. You will also need coloured paper for students to record their knowledge; this will be stuck onto the totem pole.

As a whole class, outline which topic you are going to revise. Divide the class into groups of two or three and allocate each group a chunk of the topic. The first task is to create two revision resources – a one-sided leaflet summarising their topic chunk, and a visual representation of this including a one-sentence summary. When they have made their resources, the groups place their visual representations on the totem pole and stick their information leaflets on the board. Each group can feedback to the rest of the class, summarising what they have contributed to the totem pole. After this, students can write a summary using the leaflets and the totem pole to support their learning.

Students can also complete this activity in groups, but in this instance the totem pole they create should be no more than a metre in length. Consider allocating each group a smaller topic to revise or an exam question each, for which they can use a totem pole to show their intended essay plan.

#Revisiontotempole

Visual Hexagons

It all fits together!

Visual hexagons help students to see their revision topics more clearly and make links between the obvious and the obscure.

Using hexagons within a revision programme has been covered in Idea 65. This adaption can be extremely effective and very popular with students. Visual hexagons has the same objective as the initial hexagon task but allows all students, regardless of ability, to access the higher-order skills more effectively.

Visual hexagons have a fixed pattern, with images relating to a central question or topic in each hexagon. You can find an example in the online resources.

The first stage is for students to identify the images and how they relate to the central question. The images can represent not only a specific person or event but also a larger point that may summarise an aspect that links to the set question. Once students are clear about each image, they can complete the main task, which is to explain each link between the images where the sides of the hexagons touch.

These visual hexagon activities can provide students with a great visual learning aid, which gives the hooks to prompt memory as well as being an attractive summary of a topic or question within students' notes.

Extend this task by asking the class further questions to promote thinking, such as:

- what other images can fit in the middle of the pattern?
- what other images could be used in the pattern?
- if you had to replace one image from the pattern, which one would you remove?

Teaching tip

Making visual hexagon resources using a Word document can be a laborious business. To save time, use a picture-framing app, such as Moldiv, which has ideal frames that can be easily adjusted to make bespoke resources you can use time and time again.

Taking it further

To add competition and engagement, this can be completed in pairs under a time limit. Once the time runs out, hold a class discussion where each pair shares their links and students can fill in any links they have missed or write improved ones from others.

#Visualhex

Graphic organisers for revision

Seeing is believing.

Rearranging information into a visual format is a powerful way to learn key information about a topic. The following techniques all help students to get information into their heads and also create a handy revision aid to take away.

Venn diagrams Perhaps the most well-known form of graphic representation of material, Venn diagrams are two or three overlapping circles that organise similarities and differences for a given set of criteria. Each circle represents a different category relating to an overall topic or question. Students are given a range of ideas, factors, features or terms that relate to at least one of the categories in the circles. They should place each named item in the appropriate circle or circles.

Comparison alley A similar method to a Venn diagram, advocated by David Didau, is the comparison alley. The main benefit of the comparison alley is that it gives more room than a Venn diagram to compare and contrast information.

The comparison alley looks like this:

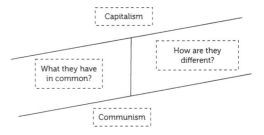

With more room for comparison this helps stretch and challenge students in your lessons.

Carroll diagrams Carroll diagrams help organise information to show if it is or isn't something. A simple version contains only two types of criteria, such as 'Prime ministers' and 'Not prime ministers'.

A more complex Carroll diagram could include an element of judgement and other categories:

	Reigned less than 20 years	Reigned longer than 20 years
Great	Richard I Henry V	Henry VIII Elizabeth I Elizabeth II
Not great	John Anne William II	Charles II

Thinking squares These allow students to record information that is stepped from identifying onto describing, to analysis onto hypothesis and are naturally differentiated and allows for students to identify relevant information and link it to exam style questions and deeper thinking.

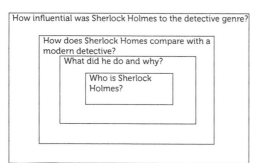

How influential was Sherlock Holmes to the detective genre?

How does Sherlock Homes compare with a modern detective?

What did he do and why?

Who is Sherlock Holmes?

Bonus idea ★

Continuums
Continuums are a great way for students to record judgements on specific issues that require consideration of a number of factors. A Continuum is a straight line with opposing criteria at each end. Students place given items that relate to the overall question where they think they fit on the continuum. This provides an effective way of ordering information and testing thinking skills. The activity can be easily differentiated if you vary the number of items you give to students, or by giving students an incomplete list and asking them to add other items that they think are relevant.

#Graphicorg

99

Foldables for revision

Fold and seek . . .

Hiding information beneath flaps of paper is more exciting and effective than it sounds.

Foldables for revision has become an online phenomenon. Search 'foldables' online and you will find a myriad of ideas using paper to create 3D graphic organisers. These are ideal for kinaesthetic learners.

All you need is lots of coloured paper! Using colour can help trigger the memory when using the foldable. It is a good idea to practise folding a foldable. There are plenty of great shapes and ideas online, with excellent Pinterest boards and tweets showing some excellent examples to emulate. To begin with fold a piece of A4 paper in half, then cut one half into strips, leaving the other half untouched. On each strip, students can write a keyword, a simple revision knowledge question or key event or person. Students then write the corresponding piece of information – definition, answer to the question or event or date that matches the event or date written – underneath the strip, so when they look at the information on the strip they can lift it up to reveal the answer.

Other foldables include:

- cut out a chain of concertina people. On each one, write the name of a person relevant to a specific topic. Include information how each person is linked to the next person in the chain.
- give students two pieces of paper. On one piece of paper ask them to cut out ten doors, number them, and then stick the cut-out onto the second piece of paper. Underneath the doors, students write their top ten facts of a topic in order of significance.

Taking it further

With the strips foldable idea, ask each student to create a strips foldable with just the key fact, question, date or event written on each strip. Students then swap their foldable with somebody else and have to write the information underneath the strips of their partner's foldable.

#Fold4revision

Revision games

Part 6

Keyword bingo

Full house!

Bingo can be modified to engage students as part of an effective revision programme.

Bingo is a straightforward, simple game that most students know. It can be used to test knowledge in a quick and easy way, and ensure students are engaged in revision sessions.

The game tests knowledge of keywords and their definitions. Get your students to draw a bingo card – it can have as many squares as you see fit. On the board write down a number of key words; there must be more words than squares on the bingo cards. Ask your students to fill in their bingo card with one key word in each square. Once this has been done you are ready to play. Call 'eyes down' and start to read definitions or descriptions of the key words from the board in random order. Students cross off the words on their card when they think the matching definition has been read out. Once a student declares a 'full house', they must read back the terms and their definitions from their full bingo card. If the rest of the class agrees that they are all correct, they are the winner! If not, the game continues until a student correctly declares a 'full house'.

Key word bingo can be altered to reflect how difficult you want to make it. For example, you can increase or decrease the number of squares within the grid. Also consider the clues you give the students. Instead of reading out definitions, you might want to give more demanding questions reflecting the exam, or make the clues more abstract.

#Revbingo

Buy your exam tips

How many exam tips can I get for a pound?

This activity will encourage your students to consider a range of exam tips and to think about what will be useful for them.

For this activity you will need some fake money, such as Monopoly money, and need to create a list of 15 to 20 exam tips, with advice such as:

- get to the exam early;
- look at how many marks each question is worth;
- plan your answer before writing it.

To cut the work down, you can either ask students in the year above to come up with a list of tips for you or, at the beginning of the activity, have a brainstorm discussion where students list their own exam tips, which you can record on the board for future reference.

The activity should be conducted with students working in groups of three, four or five. Give each group some fake money to the value of 100 pounds and a list of exam tips.

In their groups students discuss the value of the exam tips on the list and which tips they would they spend their money on. Each group can buy eight tips in total, with the values of three tips priced at £20, three tips at £10 and two at £5. Providing the students with this financial framework gives them the opportunity to decide how much the tips they have chosen are worth, and therefore automatically means that each group will have to prioritise their chosen tips in order of value and importance.

Conclude the activity with a feedback plenary session where each group presents what tips they have bought and why they have bought them.

#Selltips

103

Card games

I see your oxygen and raise you with hydrogen . . .

Revision card games can provide an engaging way of revising and break the tension of more demanding activities while still keeping the focus on exams and applying knowledge.

These card games test students' knowledge, improve their memory skills and encourage peer assessment. After guidance, students can make their own cards, which can be used in a variety of ways both in class and at home.

Each of the following games requires a pack of 20 to 30 cards, each showing a key term, event, process, character, person, year or symbol relating to the same topic.

Guess What? This game can be played in groups or pairs. Start with the cards placed face down. The first player takes the top card and the partner or group must ask questions to guess what is on the card. The first player can only answer 'yes' or 'no'. Once the item has been correctly guessed, the turn passes onto the next player. To make it more challenging, set a limit on the number of questions and/or the time taken to correctly guess the item.

Under pressure! Place the cards face down. The first player takes the top card and describes what is on the card. They have a limited amount of time to do this. If the item is guessed correctly the card is handed over to the guesser, if not the card is returned to the bottom of the pack. Students take turns in guessing until the pack is finished, and the person with the most cards wins. Alternatively, students can work in teams to see how many terms can be worked through in a set time. The team that can get through the most terms wins.

#Revcardgames

Connect Four

Linking learning has never been so engaging.

The structure of Connect Four makes an engaging revision game.

Everyone remembers the game Connect Four where you take it in turns to put different coloured counters in the frame with the aim of getting four counters of the same colour in a row. The broad principles can easily be applied to make an engaging revision game that can aid memory and recall while testing knowledge. You need a grid of six squares by five squares; in each square there is something that tests a students' knowledge on a connected topic. This could be:

- a straightforward question;
- a piece of information, such as a person, a year or a symbol whose relevance to the overall topic needs to be explained;
- a short task to demonstrate knowledge – for example, mime a key feature of a character, complete a sum or draw your learning.

Students play in threes, with two students playing the game and the third acting as referee and timekeeper, checking that the answers are correct. The playing students take it turns to try to take control of a square by answering the question or completing the task set in a given time period. If a student is correct they can colour in the square in their chosen colour. If incorrect, the square is left as it is. The aim is to get four squares in a row in your colour.

This activity relies on a children's game that most of your students will know, meaning that you save time on explaining the task. It can be adapted for practically any subject and any topic requiring written assessment and knowledge recall.

Teaching tip

The Connect Four grids can take a little time to set up at first. For inspiration, you may want to use some of the ideas from 'Find someone . . .' (Idea 18) which uses similar activities. Once you have established the game with your class, ask students to create their own grids, giving you an electronic copy so you can build a bank of Connect Four grids with subsequent classes.

Taking it further

This can also be used as a whole-class activity. Project a grid onto the board and split the class into two teams. To stretch and challenge the more able students, a pair could be appointed as referees; they have to check the answers given by the class. This is a fun way of checking knowledge and progress involving the whole class.

#Connect4rev

Crocodile creek

This is the snappiest revision activity in the book!

This activity, created by Isabella Wallace and Leah Kirkman, is brilliant for getting students to make links between their learning. It is ideal for any teacher's revision toolkit, as it also gets students to talk and apply their knowledge.

Students can work in pairs or groups for this activity. They will need a grid like the one below to represent a crocodile-infested creek.

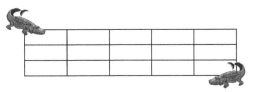

The aim of the activity is to move a counter across the river, row by row, by selecting one square from each of the rows. Each chosen square must link with the previous one in order to make a successful passage across.

Students must their blank creek information they need to revise. So for example, a crocodile creek on the Cold War could look like this:

Successful routes across the creek could be Churchill – 1946 – Iron Curtain or Roosevelt – 1945 – Yalta.

Once the students have played crocodile creek in their pairs or groups, challenge them by setting a target of how many links they need to make. Students can share the different links they have made in a plenary, you should get an amazing number of links. Sharing enhances the revision process and allows you to take a step back while students teach each other.

#Crocodilecreekrev

Faster, higher, stronger

The option is yours . . .

This interactive activity helps students to engage with exam questions and places application of knowledge right at the forefront.

Play this activity as a whole-class exercise. You will need four cards for each student with Stronger, Faster, Higher and Boycott on them, and PowerPoint slides showing exam questions. It works best for questions requiring short or medium answers.

Start by presenting an exam question slide to students. For example, 'Explain why the USSR blockaded Berlin in 1948. Give at least two reasons in your answer. *(6 marks)*'. Set a time limit for students. Before answering, students play one of their cards. They choose which one based on how they feel about the question – they can only play each card once. They write their choice at the top of their paper, before writing their answer. The meanings of the cards are:

- **Faster** Students must finish before the time limit is up for an extra mark.
- **Higher** Students score one extra mark for every mark earned in their answer.
- **Stronger** Students request an alternative question that is more difficult that then original, or has an added which would be worth double the marks.
- **Boycott** Students opt out of the question and instead revise and make notes on the question topic.

When the time limit is up, students swap their answers and mark them using guidance from you, allocating marks in accordance to the answer and the card that has been played.

#FSH

Guess who?

Is it Harry Truman?

This activity is inspired by the board game of the same name. It is great to sharpen students' memory, recall and questioning skills in an accessible and engaging way.

For this activity you need grids of nine squares with images or key words in them. These can be printed and handed out to students or it can be projected onto the board. An example, about the origins of the Cold War, is:

Iron Curtain	Josef Stalin	Yalta
Soviet Expansion	Berlin Crisis	Harry Truman
Containment	Potsdam	NATO

Students secretly select one square from the grid. With their revision partner they take turns to ask each other 'yes' and 'no' questions. The aim is to guess which square their partner has chosen using the fewest questions possible.

This challenges students to think about what makes each word or image in the grid unique from the others, how words and images can be grouped together, and the properties of each one. It can prompt deep thinking, which can be teased out in class discussion with such questions as:

- Which word or image was the most challenging to guess? Why do you think that is?
- Which word or image was the easiest to guess? Why do you think that is?
- Which word or image did you understand the most? Which word or image did you least understand?

#Guesswhorev

108

Make it! Draw it! Mime it! Act it!

How many ways can I show my revision?

This interactive game includes all the key learning styles and allows students to show their learning in a whole host of ways.

You will need a collection of craft materials and objects, such as plasticine, coloured paper, paper clips and cocktail sticks, and a set of four cards, one each for 'Make it!', ' Draw it!', 'Mime it!' and 'Act it!'. Alternatively, you could have each of the four instructions on a random name generator, such as the ones found on triptico.co.uk. You will also need a second set of cards with keywords and items of knowledge from the revision topic typed on them.

This activity can be carried out as a whole class, in two teams, or in smaller groups.

Start by asking one student to choose a keyword card and then an instruction card. The student has to make the rest of the group guess what is on the keyword card, using the method on the instruction card. For example, if the instruction card is 'Mime it!' and the keyword card says 'the Berlin Wall', the student must attempt to mime clues to help others guess.

This task can be varied in a number of ways:

- place a time limit on guessing what is on the keyword card;
- set a time limit for each student to see how many cards they can get through;
- allocate different points to keyword cards; the more difficult they are, the more points they are worth. This builds a level of differentiation into the activity.

Taking it further

Once your students are used to the activity, ask them to make up their own instruction and keyword card sets for different revision topics and swap them with others.

#Makedrawmimeact

109

Revision trumps

Fancy a game, Sir!

The principle of Top Trumps can be deftly transferred to make a revision game that requires analysis, evaluation and the application of knowledge.

For those unfamiliar with Top Trumps, it is a trading card game which is made up of a pack of trumps cards that share a common theme, such as sports cars or cowboys. Each card in the pack is about an item within the common theme and shows a list of data in a set of criteria for that item. For example, a pack based on Kings and Queens of England might show data about length of reign, age, number of children, wars won and success rating.

To start the game, deal out all the cards dealt between the players. Each player must look at the first card in their pack without showing it to any other player. Player one chooses a category they think will outscore the other players' cards and calls out the criteria and their score. The other players must call out their score for that category – the player with the highest score wins the round. The winner takes the other players' cards and adds them to the bottom of their pack.

The winner of the previous round chooses the category and calls out their score. The game continues until one player has the entire pack.

This game requires exam-related skills of analysis, evaluation and prediction, as players need to assess the data on their cards and decide how strong each piece of information is.

#Revisiontrumps

Word splat!

Beat your revision!

This rapid fire activity is ideal for kinaesthetic students and creates great energy while revising and reviewing learning. It has been advocated by Caroline Bentley-Davies, Isabelle Wallace and Leah Kirkman and can energise any revision session.

This activity revises knowledge in a light-hearted manner, and enables students to review their learning while improving their memory skills. You need a list of between 15 and 20 key terms, which can be either displayed on the board (for a whole-class activity) or written on sheets of A3 paper (for a group activity). You will also need flyswatters or a similar non-harming hitting object with which students can 'splat' their chosen words.

For a whole-class activity, divide your class into two teams with a nominated runner, who will have a flyswatter. Ask a question for which the answer is one of the words on the board. The runners race to the board from the back of the class to splat the correct answer with their flyswatter. The student who provides the fastest correct answer wins a point for their team and retains their flyswatter while the student who comes second has to hand over the flyswatter to someone else in their team.

To carry out the activity in groups of three or four, give each group a sheet showing all the relevant terms, and a flyswatter. They play the activity of 'splatting' the correct words in the same way, but also take turns to ask the questions.

Teaching tip

To prevent a few students from dominating the activity, limit the number of times they can 'splat' a word.

A useful revision homework activity would be to produce a PowerPoint slide of key words to be used in word splat for a subsequent lesson.

Taking it further

Another application as a whole-class activity could be to post the words in different parts of the room so that students have to search for the answer to 'splat' it with their flyswatter. You could place words on windows, doors and furniture such as cupboards. This application taps into the idea of the locus memory techniques (see Idea 56 – 'Context dependent learning') where words and terms can be associated with places and objects to aid the memory.

#Splat

Technology and revision

Part 7

Apps for revision

Apps to help you apply your learning when revising.

Mobile technology is an essential feature in many of our young people's lives. Many schools are now embracing mobile technology and including it as part of teaching and learning — including revision.

Here are some of the best apps that can help and encourage revision:

Popplet An app that allows students to create attractive spider diagrams and mind maps using words and images, which helps them to organise notes and ideas in a visual manner.

Revise Better Organised by subject, this app contains a wealth of quizzes, facts and flashcards to help students revise and prepare for GCSEs.

Grafio A brilliant app for creating infographics, organising and brainstorming ideas and creating visual aids, such as mind maps.

Prezi A presentation tool that helps create presentations with a limited amount of text. Use this with older students. It requires them to cut the material down to the essentials.

Audioboo An app that provides a platform to create and store audio files of revision notes which can be shared with others.

Trading Cards An app in which you can create Trump cards, summarising key information on any subject.

Evernote This allows students to store and organise revision notes and synchronise them with other mobile devices.

Studyblue This app allows students to create and share electronic flashcards and use them in quizzes to help test and memorise knowledge.

Infographics

Information – and revision – is beautiful.

Infographics are everywhere. They can be the most beautiful revision, as well as the most informative, in your revision toolkit.

An infographic is a poster or other visual representation of essential information, such as key facts, dates or statistics. They use a whole range of different ways to communicate information, such as charts, graphs, images and shapes, and have become an extremely popular, attractive and accessible way of displaying information.

To find infographics try good.is/infographics and bbc.co.uk. These sites cover a huge range of subjects. They can be used as an initial resource for a revision session, where students have to disseminate the information presented and apply it in an exam context, such as describing how it links to a specific question or topic.

Creating your own revision resources is a brilliant way to achieve active and deep learning. Asking students to create their own infographics can provide an engaging activity that produces a valuable revision aid. Here are some ideas:

- give a list of ways to display information – graphs, images and charts, for example – and ask students to use at least two of these;
- allow students to work in groups to produce an infographic on different elements of a topic which can be shared in a plenary at the end of a revision session;
- although trusty board pens and sugar paper can work well, if you have access to tablets do take time to explore the myriad of infographic maker apps.

Teaching tip

If you are going to use this activity with your students it is very useful to have infographics on display so that you can make reference to how the information is presented and what techniques can be used in them.

Taking it further

Try creating your own infographic on a topic but leave gaps for your students to fill in. This could be either concrete information, such as dates, or statistical information where students may need to make an educated guess; this can provide for good discussion work afterwards. This allows students to engage with material quickly.

Bonus idea ★

David McCandless' books **Information is Beautiful** and **Knowledge is Beautiful** contain some superb infographic resources, particularly for A Level subjects such as economics and politics.

#Revisioninfograph

Padlet

This is the only notice board I read, sir . . .

Padlet is an online notice board creator that many teachers use; it can be a key part of an effective revision programme.

In Padlet you can create simple online notice boards with specific themes. To post on a Padlet notice board, you need to click on the relevant icon; a notice similar to a post-it note appears. You can type a note of up to 160 characters in length, and within this attach links to resources, images and video. The notices on the board can be arranged in a timeline or randomly. When you create a notice board, give it a clear heading so your students know its purpose.

Padlet can be used in many ways, both inside and outside your classroom; here are a few suggestions:

- **Revision questions board** Create a Padlet board for students to post questions about their revision and for you to then respond to. The whole class can see the answer, and students do not have to wait to ask you in the next lesson.
- **Topic resource area** If you find a useful video or documentary online, post a link on the Padlet board for your students to see.
- **Group discussion board** Pose a question as the title of the Padlet board. Ask every student in the class to respond with an opinion and explanation. Great to check understanding and a challenge for students to respond in 160 characters or fewer.

You can use a password lock to ensure safety of your notice boards, just remember to share the password and link to the board with your students.

#Padlet4rev

Podcasts

Listen up . . . revision materials you can take anyway and play anytime.

Podcasts are a ubiquitous audio resource that can be accessed at all times for students both in and out of the classroom.

A podcast can be played on a website or downloaded to a mobile device. It is easy to create them using apps such as Garageband, or a digital voice recorder with USB; they can be hosted on platforms such as Audioboo for students to access. As a revision resource, podcasts are extremely flexible. Here are a few suggestions about how they can be included in your revision armoury.

- Record revision briefings focusing on a specific topic. Include key areas, important terms, issues and crucial facts, summarising the topic succinctly and accessibly.
- Record exam advice that focuses on how to answer a specific question, such as sentence starters references to the mark scheme.
- Record revision advice that pinpoints effective revision habits. Include points about how to structure and plan revision and ideas about coping with stress.
- Record podcasts that focus on reaching a specific level, such as how to go from a grade D in the mocks to a grade C in the final exam.

Consider these points when making podcasts:

- Make them 3 or 4 minutes long.
- Make the podcast objectives clear in the introduction.
- Explain how the podcast is relevant.
- Include extra reading suggestions.
- Summarise the key points at the end.

Teaching tip

This is very much a long-term revision strategy and can be time consuming. If you decide to create a library of revision podcasts, think about sharing the burden within the department. When you host them on the VLE or an alternative platform, ensure that you create clear, easy to recognise titles for each podcast, as well as writing some text to explain the key points of the podcast for easy reference and recording.

#Revpodcasts

Twitter

Tweet . . . tweet!

Twitter is the fastest growing social media platform in the world, with an estimated 300 million users in 2014. It can easily be used to enhance your revision programme.

Twitter is arguably one of the most important developments in education in the 21st century. Its ability to link educators across the world has encouraged teachers to share ideas, resources and opinions on a wider platform. For many teachers it has become 'an alternative staffroom', where they go for inspiration while building a worldwide PLN of dedicated professionals.

The power and resources of Twitter can be harnessed in many ways. Here are just a few:

- Search for specific ideas and keywords to find information and resources. Use the hashtag symbol with the word that you are looking for. Hashtags are used to group linked tweets, making them easier to locate.
- Observe and/or participate in an online discussion where teaching pearls of wisdom are shared. The most popular is #ukedchat which takes place every Thursday between 8pm and 9pm. On UK EdChat's website (ukedchat.com) there is a repository of all the chats that have taken place. These are well worth browsing as many contain brilliant teaching ideas.
- There are many subject and topic specific Twitter accounts that you can encourage students to follow. For example @Amazingmaps for geographers, @Deutschhappen for German speakers and @coldwarhistory for students studying the Cold War.
- Students can also tweet your department account to ask questions relating to their revision. Give them a hashtag to use so you can locate and archive their tweets.

Teaching tip

When using a Twitter account that can be accessed by your students, make it as transparent as possible to others by sharing it with colleagues, including the headteacher. In the account profile include a disclaimer that it does not represent any personal opinions and ensure that the account is advertised to all within the school community, including parents. For additional security, you may wish to lock the account so you can monitor who follows you and accesses your tweets more closely.

Taking it further

Create a personal account for your own teaching research and a department account for students to follow; use the latter to promote the good work of your students and share revision information that students can access at any time, anywhere. Tweet reminders for exam dates, links to useful revision websites, celebrations of quality work and revision tips.

#Twit4rev

Word clouds

Your revision can reach the sky with word clouds.

Word clouds are a popular way of presenting key words and themes and can make striking visual learning resources.

Word clouds are very easy to make and there are plenty of examples you can grab off the internet. tagxedo.com online and the app Phoetic allow you to make word clouds in different shapes, and make particular words larger to highlight their significance. You can make word clouds from speeches in the shape of the person who made them, or lyrics in the shape of the singer, or key words for a topic in shapes that relate to the topic.

Word clouds can be used in a variety of ways in a revision session, such as:

- ask students to pick three words from the word cloud and explain their significance to what they have revised;
- ask students to justify why some words are bigger than others in the word cloud;
- ask students to create a sentence summarising what they have revised using at least three words used in the word cloud.

However, the best way to use word clouds is getting students to create their own.

- Students write 20 words summarising a topic.
- Ask students to underline the 4 most important words, in their opinion, out of the 20 they have just written.
- Students then choose a person or object that best sums up the topic.
- Students create their word clouds in their exercise book using their 20 chosen words, with the 4 top words being the largest in the word cloud and using the chosen image or person as the shape of their word cloud.

Teaching tip

Before using word clouds in your revision lesson, explore how to make them yourself and provide students with examples so they know what they are trying to create.

Taking it further

You could flip the use of word clouds in your revision session by presenting students with a completed word cloud and asking them to identify the topic the words relate to and why. This would make an excellent starter to a revision session.

#Revisionwordclouds

Embrace new technologies

Young people spend so much time online. I capitalise on this when designing their revision activities.

Incorporating new technologies into your students' revision activities allows for a rich and engaging experience, whatever the subject matter or the age of the students. Here are some ways to use new technologies to create revision materials.

- Quizzes are a fantastic tool for students to assess their level of existing knowledge. Sites such as Socrative, SAM Learning and YacaPaca allow you to set your students quizzes on a range of topics, choosing from pre-existing quizzes or authoring your own. You can then monitor your students' performance and plan additional teaching as necessary. Alternatively, BBC Bitesize has a range of revision resources including quizzes that students can access without the need for login details. These make handy starters, plenaries and homework tasks.
- There are several interactive whiteboard apps available for tablets that allow teachers to record their drawings, complete with an audio explanation. This is an excellent way to create revision materials for your students that will help them to recap key concepts and techniques outside of lessons. The recordings can be uploaded to the Internet as video files which the students can access from anywhere. Educreations is a free app and provides a good starting point.
- There is a wealth of multimedia resources available online which can help students to visualise difficult concepts, or allow them to put what they are learning in a wider context. Sites such as YouTube and TeacherTube have an extensive range of videos that you can build into your students' revision activities.

#Newtech4rev

Get your students revising online

I can take my revision with me wherever I go.

These ideas will allow students to revise from their laptops, tablets or smartphones at home or on the go. This way students can revise little and often, whenever and wherever they like.

- As you go through the year, get one student per week to sum-up the week's learning up as an entry on a class blog. By the end of the year you will have an excellent online revision resource that the students can access from a range of devices. Sites such as Edublogs and Kidblog are perfect for this because they are specifically set up for educational use.
- New technology provides a number of opportunities for students to collaborate. Using online tools, such as Google Drive, students can produce shared revision guides, glossaries or essay plans. You could even get them to share the links to these documents with you.
- There are several online mind-mapping tools that allow students to display their knowledge of a topic and its interconnections visually. The mind maps can then be saved and shared between students. Popplet and bubbl.us are two popular examples of mind mapping websites that could be used for this purpose.
- To jazz up your revision programme, ask your students to present a topic in the form of a comic strip or animation. Websites such as Chogger and Powtoon allow produce great results and do not require any artistic or technical abilities!
- Remind students that they can access past exam papers and mark schemes online; some exam boards have made these available via apps for smartphones and tablets.

Teaching tip

The beauty of online revision resources is that parents can access them too! Consider providing parents with a list of the online revision resources that you have recommended to your students. Parents will welcome the opportunity to see what their children are up to, and may even be better equipped to support the revision themselves as a result

#Onlinerevision

121

Bibliography

The activities included in this book have come from a wide range of resources and influences and I have tried to acknowledge the main influences throughout. However, I have found the following books and resources especially useful in improving my teaching and the learning of my students. I hope they do the same for you.

Books

J. Ahrenfelt and N. Watkin, *The Exam Class Toolkit*, (Continuum, 2010)

M. Anderson, Perfect ICT Every Lesson, (Independent Thinking Press, 2013)

P. Beadle, *How to Teach*, (Crown House, 2010)

J. Beere, *The Perfect OFSTED Lesson*, (Independent Thinking Press, 2nd edition, 2012)

C. Bentley-Davies, *Outstanding Lessons*, (Teachers' Pocketbooks, 2011)

C. Bentley-Davies, *Literacy Across the Curriculum*, (Teachers' Pocketbooks, 2013)

S. Bowkett, *100 Ideas for Teaching Thinking Skills*, (Continuum, 2006)

K. Brown, *Classroom Starters and Plenaries*, (Continuum, 2009)

S. Chapman et al., *Improving Classroom Performance*, (Crown House, 2012)

S. Cottrell, *The Exam Skills Handbook*, (Palgrave, 2007)

S. Cottrell, *The Study Skills Handbook*, (Palgrave, 3rd edition, 2009)

D. Didau, *The Perfect English OFSTED Lesson*, (Independent Thinking Press, 2012)

D. Didau, *The Secret of Literacy*, (Independent Thinking Press, 2014)

C. Gadsby, *Perfect Assessment for Learning*, (Independent Thinking Press, 2012)

M. Gershon, *More Secondary Starters and Plenaries*, (Bloomsbury, 2013)

M. Gershon, *Secondary Starters and Plenaries – History*, (Bloomsbury, 2013)

P. Ginnis, *The Teacher's Toolkit*, (Crown House, 2001)

D. Grey, *Getting the Buggers to Learn*, (Continuum, 2006)

A. Griffith and M. Burns, *Engaging Learners*, (Crown House, 2012)

A. Griffith and M. Burns, *Teaching Backwards*, (Crown House, 2014)

T. Haward, *Seeing History*, (Network Education Press, 2005)

D. Hodgson and T. Benton, The Brain Box, (Crown House, 2014)

N. Jackson, *The Little Book of Music for the Classroom*, (Crown House, 2009)

D. Keeling and D. Hodgson, *Invisible Teaching*, (Crown House, 2011)

W. Kidd and G. Czerniawski, *Teaching Teenagers*, (Sage 2011)

L. Kirkman and I. Wallace, *Pimp Your Lesson!* (Continuum, 3rd edition, 2014)

L. Kirkman and I. Wallace, *Talk-Less Teaching*, (Crown House, 2014)

G. Long, H. Grout and S. Taylor, *101 Classroom Games*, (Human Kinetics, 2011)

E. Lunzer and K. Gardner, *The Effective use of Reading*, (1979, Heinemann)

G. Luzet, *Collaborative Learning Pocketbook*, (Teachers' Pocketbook, 2013)

J. Smith, *The Lazy Teacher's Handbook*, (Crown House, 2010)

J. Smith, *Follow Me I'm Right Behind You: Whole School Progress the Lazy Way*, (Independent Thinking Press, 2012)

University of the First Age, *Brain Friendly Revision*, (UFA, 2002)

University of the First Age, *Learning BITES*, (UFA, 2008)

D. Walker Tileston, *Teaching Strategies for Active Learning*, (Corwin Press 2007)

E-books

M. Cowan, *Techniques for Top Teaching*, (2012)

W. Emeny, *100 Things Awesome Teachers Do*, (2012)

P. MacMurray, *Study Skills Essentials – Oxford Graduates Reveal Their Study Tactics, Essay Secrets and Exam Advice*, (2011)

M. Smith, *30 Ways to Get Your A Level Students Working Harder Than You*, (2014)